D0467192

How to Find Fish—
and Make Them Strike

Also by Joseph D. Bates, Jr.

Spinning for American Game Fish

Trout Waters and How to Fish Them

Streamer Fly Fishing in Fresh and Salt Water

Spinning for Fresh Water Game Fish

Spinning for Salt Water Game Fish

The Outdoor Cook's Bible

Streamer Fly Tying and Fishing

Elementary Fishing

Atlantic Salmon Flies and Fishing

Reading the Water

Fishing

An Outdoor Life Book

How to Find Fish— and Make Them Strike

by Joseph D. Bates, Jr.

with Water-Reading Photos by Rex Gerlach

OUTDOOR LIFE / HARPER & ROW

NEW YORK, EVANSTON, SAN FRANCISCO, LONDON

Manufactured in the United States of America

Contents

1

The Basics of Finding Fish

There is a saying that "ten percent of the fishermen catch ninety percent of the fish," and although this statistic has never been verified, a germ of truth is lodged in the assertion. Whatever the percentage of anglers who come home fishless more often than not, it is a large group, most of whose members have one thing in common: slight knowledge of the habits of their quarry. The purpose of this book is to enlarge that knowledge and to help readers join that "ten percent" who catch most of the fish.

In order to catch fish, we first have to find them, and this is where we begin our study. Anglers generally go about finding fish in one of three ways.

Those who fish an area often learn the choicest locations, the quietly flowing water behind a certain rock, the dark current by an undercut bank, the sanctuary of submerged roots below a dead tree. These places remain good because new fish move into them after others have been caught. The trouble with this method is that the angler is at a disadvantage when he fishes new territory.

Another method is fishing by eyesight. Though this can be done while wading, or while sitting in a slowly moving boat, it is best done by remaining in one place and observing the water. We may see a feeding fish rise from behind a midstream rock, or the slight dimple it makes when sucking in an insect. Since the fish occupies a certain lie, into which it periodically settles, it may come up from this position again and again.

In eyesight fishing the angler looks for faint signs of fish—a shape near the bottom, or a slight movement as a fish alters its position. He may notice a slight swirl, a head-and-tail rise, a tailing only, or some similar indication of feeding fish. To the expert, various types of rises not only indicate the presence of fish, but also what they are feeding on, as we shall learn later. On lakes and ponds, the flurry of small baitfish breaking the surface tells us that gamefish are feeding from below. Tiny dimples in a windrow or wind edge tell us that gamefish (or baitfish) are sipping insects on the surface. Unusual motion in lily-pad areas indicates where bass are feeding in the shallows. These are only a few examples.

Some anglers become adept at eyesight fishing, while to others the faint signs of gamefish mean nothing. The ability to perceive fish is acquired by experience; it comes easier to some people than to others. Try to develop this ability, because it can be combined with other methods of finding fish.

The third method is the ability to "read the water," and it is the best one because it can be applied anywhere. Future chapters in this book will develop this method as it applies to various species in lakes or streams. Reading the water is the ability to instinctively select the few good locations from the many poor or fishless ones. It is the ability to "think like a fish," knowing the hiding places that fish seek for themselves.

During my apprentice years as a beginner in angling I was fortunate to have been included on various fishing trips with great anglers such as Herbie Welch, Bill Edson and Joe Stickney, all of whom have passed to their reward. These older anglers had obtained by experience an uncanny ability to "read the water," a proficiency also ingrained in other renowned experts such as Gordon, Hewitt, La Branche and Skues, to mention only a few. All of them took time to "read the water" before they fished it, and to plan the strategy of their approach before making the first cast.

I remember the day in my youth when Herbie Welch, an angling crony of former President Herbert Hoover, took me fishing on then-famous Kennebago Stream, in Maine. On arriving at one of the best pools I promptly waded in and started casting. Herbie remained sitting on the bank, quietly smoking his pipe. Since the slight frown on his face indicated I must be doing something wrong, I waded ashore and joined him.

"Aren't you going to fish?" I asked.

"Now, you sit right down here and let me tell you a thing or two," he said. "You waded into the best part of the run and scared the fish there. You should have seen them scooting away. Before you start to fish a new spot, you should take time to study the water. Sit down and relax and look it over. You waded too close to that rock before fishing it, and I saw a good trout feeding there before you splashed in. Over there is another run you may not have disturbed. You can reach that lush green area on the far bank, where a spring trickles in—a real hot spot in the summer."

Herbie went on to explain how to read the water of the pool to select the good spots from the others. He pointed to where he would wade to cast, and how the fly should be fished in each spot. He explained the sequence of casting positions—where to start fishing the pool, and what to do next, and so on after that. From that time on we would stand or sit together in new places while I outlined the strategy of fishing them. He would correct me when I was wrong, and explain what I had missed. He taught me much about how to "read the water"—lessons never to be forgotten. We frequently would stroll along the bank to examine the stream and to plan how we would fish it. This disclosed depressions, submerged rocks and feed lanes which we might not have observed while fishing. Then we would return later, and flycast when the stream was undisturbed.

Of course all anglers can read the water to an extent. The best ones have learned by study and experience. In the next few chapters we will examine photographs of actual situations so that readers who study them can gain experience without wasting time while fishing.

Roger Woodcock for State of Maine

The author shows his wife, Helen, how to read water on a stream.

LOCATING FISH BY THEIR HABITS

Since fish don't resemble people, are cold-blooded, and live in water, most anglers don't stop to think that their requirements are more like those of people than people might presume. If we consider the requirements of fish and relate them to the water we are fishing, we can come pretty close to locating them by their habits.

While each species varies somewhat in its requirements, let's start by saying that there are five basic ones, plus the inborn urge to travel (usually once a year) to a suitable place to spawn. Fish need sufficient *oxygen* in water where they live. They want this water to be in a comfortable *temperature* range. They usually want a place to hide or rest which gives them adequate *protection*. Those in streams or other areas of fast flow seek places of moderate flow where they can rest in reasonable *comfort* without combatting currents. Finally, of course, they want abundant *food* nearby, or convenient enough so they can travel to it with minimum effort.

When we consider these five basic requirements in regard to where we are fishing it is obvious that we can eliminate certain areas, or water levels, and concentrate on the places where these five requirements are met.

There are several fine points to all this which we'll explore later, but first let's define the requirements a little more exactly.

Sufficient Oxygen

Fish need oxygen to breathe, just as we do. Oxygen is dissolved in water and is taken from it by action of the fish's gills. Those of us who live near sea level aren't comfortable at high altitudes because air contains less oxygen there. While some species of fish require more oxygen than others, we should seek them in areas containing more rather than less. In reservoirs we often see fountains of water jetting up so the water can absorb oxygen from the air. In streams, waterfalls or turbulence accomplish this naturally. On the other hand, pollution from industrial waste, sewage, and such contaminants as sawdust from lumber mills reduce the oxygen content of water, often to such an extent that gamefish can't live in it. Decaying vegetation, often found in man-made impoundments and beaver ponds, may have this effect temporarily.

Instruments are available for measuring the oxygen content of water at various depths. However, we usually know whether or not the water where we are fishing contains enough oxygen to support the kinds of fish we want to catch, so this requirement then can be eliminated. However, it is important and should be borne in mind.

Suitable Temperature Range

People like temperatures in the 70-degree range. When the air becomes too cold or too hot, we move to where it is warmer or cooler. Fish are even more particular about water temperature, being sensitive to changes as small as even a fraction of a degree. Each species seeks its ideal temperature, but can tolerate a somewhat wider range, as the Temperature-Activity Table for Freshwater Fish on page 5 indicates. A Temperature-Activity Table for Trout is included on page 122, and similar tables can be worked out for other species.

Of course fish can exist, if they have to, in water well out of their optimum (ideal) or tolerant temperature ranges, but they become more or less dormant in these uncomfortable temperatures and often won't even take bait when it is drifted in front of their noses.

This indicates that we should consider water temperatures and seek fish in the areas or depths where ideal or tolerant temperatures exist. We know, for example, that in summer bass come into the shallows to feed between dusk and daylight when the water is cooler there, but that they seek the depths during midday when surface water is too warm.

Since suitable water temperature is very important in finding fish we will deal with it to a greater extent later. Modern technology has developed instruments for locating depths at which suitable temperatures exist; the object is to determine these depths and get our bait or lure down there. Usually these depths encounter the sides of lakes, or submerged reefs or islands. In streams whose exposed areas are too warm, fish either lie deep in the cooler water of pools, or have migrated to more acceptable temperatures in cold-water brooks.

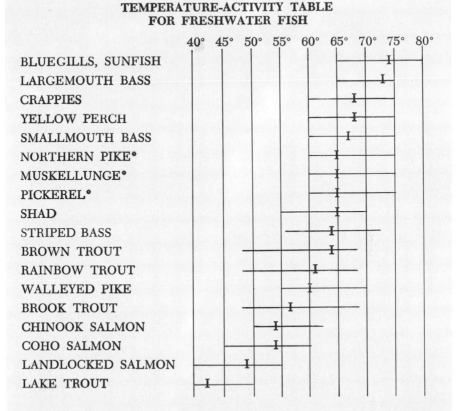

**TEMPERATURE-ACTIVITY TABLE
FOR FRESHWATER FISH**

Note: "I" indicates ideal temperature. While this may vary somewhat in various regions, this chart should be followed unless regional data suggests variation. The horizontal line indicates optimum temperature range. Fish usually will not take lures well outside of this range.

° Members of the Pike family, which includes northern pike, muskellunge and the various pickerels, are much less fussy about water temperatures than other species. While the range shown for them is the optimum one, they usually will take lures when the water is slightly warmer or very much colder.

Adequate Protection

Gamefish, except perhaps some of the anadromous species, have learned by instinct that they must hide from fishermen and predators if they are to survive. They venture from cover in search of food when they think they will be undisturbed, but remain under cover, or quickly return to it, when danger threatens. In streams, such protective cover may be the overhang of a rock in the current, the area under a ledge or a fallen tree, an undercut bank, or the depths of a pool. In lakes and ponds it may be the shady cover of lily pads or the concealment of other vegetation, submerged roots or brush piles, rocks, or the depth of the water itself.

Anglers learn to identify such places instinctively and they know that, when such places also satisfy other requirements being discussed, they are almost certain to conceal gamefish. Anadromous species such as salmon, shad and steelhead, which spend most of their lives in the ocean, have not learned to fear man and other predators to such an extent, so they often lie or cruise in sight, unmindful of the fact that anglers are plainly visible and are fishing for them.

Of course the instinct of concealment, of hiding from the eyes of predators, is more acute in some species of fish than others. Members of the trout families are particularly shy, usually fleeing for protection even when they see the flash of a rod being handled by an unseen angler. Gamefish do not always run for cover when danger threatens, but they usually will not feed and will ignore anglers' lures.

Anglers know that gamefish flee from the sound, as well as from the sight, of a man on the bank or in the water. We may find fish when we walk clumsily along a stream bank or when we noisily handle equipment in a boat, but we won't catch them. Sound waves carry long distances under water, and fish are quick to distinguish unnatural vibrations from natural ones.

Reasonable Comfort

Another similarity between the requirements of fish and of people is their desire for comfort. We dislike strong winds, so we try to stand or walk where we are protected. Fish dislike to combat strong currents, so they rest in areas of moderate flow.

What is *moderate flow?* An easy way to determine the difference between fast and moderate flow is to stand facing downstream in the fast water of a river. Put your hand in the water on either side of your boot and you'll notice that the flow of water past it will be equal in strength to the current. Put your hand in front of or directly behind the boot, however, and you will find that the flow is more moderate. Any major obstruction in a stream, such as a rock, the trunk of a fallen tree, or a jutting ledge, produces the same effect, but usually to a much greater degree. The obstruction creates an area of moderate flow in which fish like to rest; they can lie in such places with a minimum of exertion. These places are often called *holding positions.*

While doing the boot experiment, look downward where the boot's obstruction causes moderate flow, and beside the boot, where it doesn't. You will see two streaming lines in the water on each side of the moderate flow area where they meet the fast unimpeded flow. These are called *edges.* You can see them on both sides of a rock or a ledge in a stream, where a brook enters a river, where currents converge downstream of an island, and in other places that we'll illustrate in this and later chapters.

Fish like to lie inside these edges, where there is moderate flow. They look toward the faster water for food, and will flash out to take it, but they

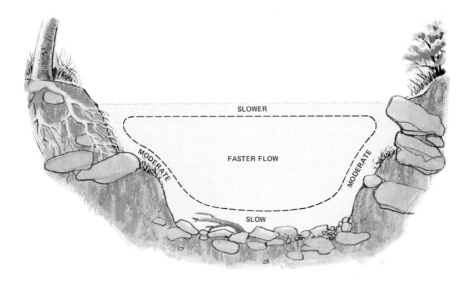

Obstructions in a stream create areas of moderate flow which fish prefer to inhabit. Moderate to slow current flows along the sides and bottom of a stream (above); the surface current is also slower than the middle. The current is always moderate behind a midstream rock (below), and fish hold inside the edges.

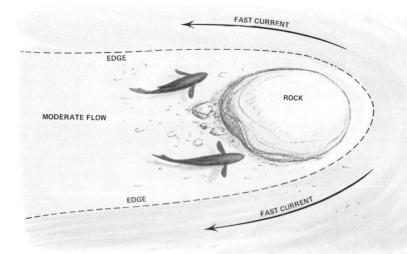

quickly return to their holding positions inside the edge in the moderate flow where they can remain in position without undue exertion.

Since obstructions in a stream cause areas of moderate flow, it is obvious that streams flow more slowly close to their banks or beds. Rocks and gravel, tree roots, vegetation and other such impediments brake the current to send the faster flow away from the banks. The slowest flow is along the stream bed, with more moderate flow along its sides. Surface water also flows a little slower than the main current.

This is one reason why gamefish usually lie along the bottom of a stream, or along its sides. Another is that protection and food are available in such places. The side that is in the shade is usually the better one for fishing.

Abundant Food

Gamefish congregate where food is easiest to find, or they travel to such places from their havens of security when they are hungry. In streams, the water reader notices feed lanes—relatively narrow, faster currents which catch food and wash it downstream. Floating objects indicate these. When a feed lane goes past a rock or other obstruction offering moderate flow, thus offering protection, comfort and food, the place should be a hot spot. Feed lanes are often seen to pass by undercut banks or protruding ledges. Such places satisfy these requirements and thus should be hot spots also. Active eddies may not offer much protection, except perhaps in deep water, but they may be cruising areas and feeding grounds for less spooky fish than trout—smallmouth bass, for example. Even trout go to such places at feeding times, largely because schools of minnows are found there.

Trout periodically leave their protective havens to feed in the tails of pools or in riffles, usually around daylight or after dusk, or even under brighter conditions when hatches of insects are emerging. Since their protective havens are at a distance then, they are wary and scoot for cover at the slightest provocation. Except when trout are seen to be rising to insects or their nymphs, most of the feeding will be on or near the bottom. In the deeper stretches of pools, the "in between" water is usually unproductive, yet this is the area where novices do most of their fishing.

Feeding habits of fish in ponds and lakes, where currents do not exist, present different problems. Since these have many facets, they will be discussed in detail in Chapter 5. Briefly, fish in ponds or lakes spend most of their time at levels where water temperatures suit them; usually where these temperature levels are near the sides of the lake, or islands, submerged reefs or ridges. From these places they travel to feeding areas in shallower water —rocky shorelines, lily pad areas, or similar places abundant in grasses and other vegetation. Fish feed at regular intervals and their travels can often be predicted. We shall see that the routes from the depths to the feeding areas are paths of migration chosen because of bottom contours which make such travel easier and safer. This gets us into the interesting and valuable details of "structure fishing," to be discussed primarily in Chapters 5 and 7.

When these five requirements are considered together we begin to understand the basic elements of finding fish. By combining the five we can begin to pinpoint the best locations, eliminating the majority of areas because they don't qualify. The "sufficient oxygen" requirement may not be pertinent if the water is relatively free of pollution and appears to be well oxygenated. The "reasonable comfort" one doesn't apply unless water is flowing. Of the other three, a "suitable temperature range" is usually most important because fish do more resting than feeding, and they rest where water temperatures are to their liking. When streams get too warm in summer, fish select the depths of pools or they run up cold-water brooks. When the near-surface water of ponds and lakes becomes too warm or too cold, fish select the depths where it is more comfortable. We will see that modern technology provides ways of determining these depths. The requirement of "abundant food" of course is important, but we will learn to find out where fish are when they aren't feeding, and we will learn how to tempt them to strike baits or lures there. The requirement of "adequate protection" is always important except in certain cases where fish leave protective cover to find food. We now know that protective cover has two meanings—the cover of hiding places which offer concealment for fish in shallow water and the cover of depth in relatively deep water. When water temperatures are suitable this depth may be fairly near the surface where water is cloudy, or much deeper where water is clear. Fish seem to think they are safe when they can't see what's going on above the surface. Thus, ordinarily, we combine the requirements of water temperature and protective cover to find fish, preferably in areas offering an adequate or abundant food supply. This narrows the good fishing places down to a relative few, while eliminating most of the others.

Let's look at six stream situations which help to illustrate the requirements of protection, comfort and food in streams. These are given here because they are basic. Other interesting situations applying to streams and lakes will be given in future chapters.

PROTECTION OF AN UNDERCUT BANK

The current edge near the right bank and the dark water there that extends downstream from the riffle indicate that the bank is undercut. The undercut bank provides both protection and shade for fish.

If the undercut bank were not there the moderate flow area caused by the tiny island (made by a fallen section of bank) might be a good holding position for trout, and in that case it should be fished carefully, particularly if there is any evidence of feeding activity in the riffle along the left edge. Since the undercut bank provides a better situation, fish should lie under it at all times. The edge on the right is so slow that all the water between the bank and the left edge should be good, but the water under the bank provides protection and food as well as comfort.

The right edge provides food, terrestrial insects which have fallen into the water upstream or from the grassy bank above. Casts should be made from the left so the fly or lure will work downstream close to the bank, under it if possible.

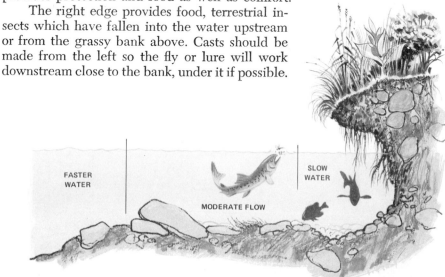

PROTECTION OF A FALLEN TREE

The current in this deep, shadowy pool runs from right to left. The partially submerged tree provides protection and shade for fish, but other good lies are below and above some of the large rocks in the pool.

Fish should lie close to the tree's branches in the deeper part of the pool, as indicated. If this tree was a bare trunk breaking the flow in the pool, fish should be hiding under the trunk in the shade of the upstream side. In such situations I have found that flies or lures must be worked close to the trunk because fish usually won't move far from its protection to take them. In fact, the take is usually when the lure almost touches the trunk or is carried under it.

Sometimes several trees have fallen into a tangle in streams, or have drifted down and been caught by an obstruction. If there is current, such spots provide hideaways for trout or smallmouth bass.

Note that there is a small eddy on the downstream side of the tree and that floating foods and bits of debris collect there. This indicates that the spot should attract minnows, so it provides food, shade and moderate flow, as well as protection.

EDGES AND MODERATE FLOW CAUSED

Recall the example of feeling the force of water flowing around your boot. There was an area of moderate flow below the boot, and the two edges it formed separated the moderate flow from the faster water of the stream. This photograph is a graphic example which is clarified in the drawing on page 7.

The edges and the area of moderate flow between them can be seen clearly in the photograph. The rock obstructs the current, providing edges and a moderate flow area. Here the edges are white water, and thus very obvious. In slower streams they may appear only as streaks caused by the differences in current flow, and may often be almost imperceptible. As the symbols show, fish habitually "hold," or rest, in the calmer water just inside the edges. Other examples of edges will be noted as we go along. When obstructions are large the area of moderate flow can also be large, holding several fish of moderate size, or perhaps one tackle buster which wants the spot all to itself. The water between the edges is several inches deeper than that in the surrounding rapids.

Other, smaller rocks can be seen which provide similar conditions, but their holding water would harbor only small fish, if any at all. Rocks in streams often overhang on the upstream or downstream sides, also providing hiding places and shade.

EDGE

MODERATE FLOW OFFERED BY A JUTTING LEDGE

This photograph provides an interesting example of moderate flow along the side of a stream. A ledge juts out from the cliff face at the left, forming a rather indistinct edge extending downstream. The moderate flow between the edge and the bank causes bits of foam to collect there, principally in the two small eddies noted on the picture. Anglers who fish this pool often find big fish holding below the two eddies, and sometimes in the other areas of moderate flow close to the bank.

Since the bank is steep we can assume that the water near it is deep; this being confirmed by its dark color. This deep stretch is ideal dry-fly water during hatches and spinner falls, but it is excellent at all times, particularly when it is in shadow. The gravel bottom can be seen in the foreground, indicating that the stretch of moderate flow near the cliff is the hot spot. Of course it should be fished from the shallow side, in the foreground.

MODERATE FLOW OFFERED BY ROCKS IN A FAST STREAM

By studying the currents we can see the quieter area of moderate flow downstream of the rock near the center of the photograph and the edges which separate the moderate flow from the full force of the current. Fish lie inside the edges, often close to the rock; but if the stream's flow is moderate, they may be inside the diminishing edges well downstream of the rock.

The disturbed surface water caused by the currents and the edges provides a degree of concealment for fish. The rock, particularly if it offers overhangs or crevices, gives added concealment. Such places, offering both protection and comfort, are excellent holding positions for fish, and the nearness of a feed lane in the fast current is another advantage.

At the lower right of this picture another big rock breaks the flow, forming another pair of edges which can be seen clearly. Thus, part of the main flow of the current is confined into a sort of chute between the adjacent edges of the two rocks. This fast current is a prominent feed lane. Fish may be anywhere between each of these two pairs of edges, the best spot being inside the edges beside the fast current feed lane. Their probable locations are noted.

FEED LANE

A PROMINENT FEED LANE THAT DOES DOUBLE DUTY

In addition to suitable water temperatures we know that the four other requirements of fish are sufficient oxygen, adequate protection, reasonable comfort and abundant food. This spot has all of them—in spades! The well-oxygenated water comes into the pool over a long, fast-flowing riffle in the foreground to concentrate its flow in a deep stretch along the far bank well protected by dense, overhanging bushes in an area where the stream's flow is slowed down by roots and branches in it. The current's direction indicates that the bank also may be somewhat undercut.

This concentration of flow along the protective cover of the bank also concentrates there various foods drifting downstream. Noting the current's direction, we presume the greatest food concentration is along the bank more to the left. However, the bushes also support abundant terrestrial foods which periodically drop into the stream, so the entire lane should be abundant.

Spots such as this are common in many areas and should provide good fishing all season. While fish may be lying under cover anywhere along the bank, the best places are indicated by symbols. Casts should be made directly to the far bank, putting the fly or lure into pockets in the overgrowth wherever possible. This is an ideal spot for fly fishermen, who usually can wade down the riffle to cast floating flies into the brushy pockets. When no hatch is in progress imitations of terrestrials such as grasshoppers and bees should bring strikes from big fish. Since the riffle is a gravel one, sunken drifting nymphs also should do well. The best time to fish this water is when the bank is in shade.

15

SPAWNING INFORMATION FOR FRESHWATER FISH

SPECIES	SPAWN IN	APPROX. WATER TEMPER- ATURE	SPAWN WHERE?
BLUEGILLS, SUNFISH	Late May to early August	65° – 70°	Sand and gravel areas with some vegetation near shorelines of ponds and lakes
LARGEMOUTH BASS	Early May to late June	62° – 70° (north) 65° – 80° (south)	Sand and gravel areas with some vegetation near shorelines of ponds and lakes
CRAPPIES	Late May to late July	60° – 70° (north) 70° – 80° (south)	Sand and gravel areas with some vegetation in water usually less than 10 feet deep
YELLOW PERCH	Mid-March to mid-May	45° – 50°	Weedy or brushy areas in shallow to deeper water of ponds and lakes (Sometimes migrate up tributaries)
SMALLMOUTH BASS	Late April to late June	59° – 65°	Sand and gravel areas 5 to 20 feet deep in lakes, ponds and streams
NORTHERN PIKE	Early spring	35° – 50°	Shallow, weedy areas of lakes; also migrate up tributaries to flooded areas
MUSKEL- LUNGE	April to June	48° – 60°	Shallow bays of lakes in muddy, stumpy bottom
PICKEREL	Early spring	45° – 50°	Weedy shoal areas of lakes, ponds or tributary streams
SHAD	November (south) to June (far north)	55° – 70°	Upper reaches of rivers with free access to ocean

SPAWNING MIGRATIONS

Earlier in this chapter another way of finding fish was noted, which is to understand their inborn urge to travel at their chosen time of year to a suitable place to spawn. The time of year varies among different species but we can locate them, often in great numbers, by understanding their spawning habits because they migrate in schools for this purpose. Let's note a few examples:

In early spring vast schools of yellow perch leave Chesapeake Bay (and many other lakes and bays) and migrate up tributary rivers to spawn. They

SPAWNING INFORMATION FOR FRESHWATER FISH

SPECIES	SPAWN IN	APPROX. WATER TEMPER- ATURE	SPAWN WHERE?
BROWN TROUT	October to February	50° – 65°	Tributary streams or rocky shallow areas of lakes
RAINBOW TROUT	Spring*	50° – 65°	Tributary streams or rocky shallow areas of lakes
WALLEYED PIKE	Spring, after ice breaks up	45° – 50°	Shoal areas of lakes or tributary streams
BROOK TROUT	September to December	48° – 55°	Small gravel brooks or gravel shorelines of lakes
CHINOOK SALMON	Nearly every month, depending on type of run	50° – 55°	Gravel areas of upper reaches of streams with free access to ocean
COHO SALMON	October to February	50° – 55°	Gravel areas of upper reaches of streams with free access to ocean
LANDLOCKED SALMON	Early October to late November	45° – 55°	Lake inlets or outlets with gravel or rubble bottom
LAKE TROUT	Early October to late November	37° – 50°	Gravel or rocky bottoms of lakes or reefs at varying depths

* Most rainbow trout spawn in the spring, the time varying with regional climatic conditions. Steelhead (anadromous rainbow trout) normally ascend rivers to spawn between October and February, but some Pacific streams have summer runs which go up much earlier.

NOTE: Geographical temperature variations prevent providing concise regional information. Consult local anglers for more accurate details about your favorite species.

do this at water temperature of about 45 degrees in the fresh and flowing water of smaller river branches often only a few feet wide and a foot or two deep. Anglers who don't know this may fish in deeper water with little or no result. Anglers who do, meet the hoards of perch upriver and land one on nearly every cast, usually using small, live minnows for bait.

In New England a red-letter fishing week occurs early in May when smelt, which have run up tributary streams from lakes and bays to spawn, return to the lakes and bays again. Trout and landlocked salmon wait for them near the stream mouths and big ones can be caught there. Anglers who understand this spawning urge can feast on succulent fried smelt as well as enjoying excellent fishing for trout and salmon. Some of the fish caught are of record size.

The annual runs of anadromous fish from the ocean up rivers to spawn are well known to anglers. The fish are usually rainbow trout (steelhead) or salmon. These runs usually occur between late fall and early spring. Some streams also have summer runs. Anglers native to a certain river know exactly when the fish should be there and which pools should be most productive as the season advances.

Brook trout that live in lakes collect around the mouths of tributary streams in the fall waiting for the spawning urge to impel them upstream when the flow and temperature of the stream is to their liking. Brown trout sometimes do the same, but are less migratory. Rainbow trout that are not anadromous are spring spawners which often go up streams then. A bit of inquiry will inform any fisherman about what's going on so he can find runs when they occur locally and enjoy prime fishing.

The table on pages 16 and 17 shows the spawning habits of most fresh water gamefish. It is necessarily general due to changing climatic conditions in various parts of the United States, but it should give fishermen an inkling of what to expect.

2

Locating Hot Spots in Rivers

Now let's examine in greater detail the various types of water found in most rivers and discuss how to fish them. We refer mainly to the various species of trout, but will also consider smallmouth bass, walleyes and other species. All of them seek fairly similar holding and feeding positions.

For maximum authenticity the majority of photographs shown were taken on important fishing rivers by a photographer accompanying an expert angler who was catching fish. Thus, when typical holding or feeding positions are marked by fish symbols as "hot spots" this means that large fish were caught there or that the positions are known to hold fish. The pictures were taken by prominent angler-author-photographer Rex Gerlach, who often used a polarized lens on his camera to reduce surface glare so we can look into the water. Such a lens corresponds to the polarized eyeglasses used in bright sunlight by knowledgeable anglers for the same purpose.

HOLDING WATER AND FEEDING WATER

Two kinds of water are shown: *holding water* where fish usually lie, or rest during travel, because it offers moderate flow plus the protection of obstructions, depth and/or the concealment of a disturbed surface; *feeding water* where fish can usually be seen in riffles, eddies, shallow parts of a gravel pool, feed lanes, or areas under bushy banks where food drops down to them. Feeding water of course is productive only during feeding periods.

These two kinds of water often offer characteristics that combine to make certain places both holding and feeding water; usually spots that provide moderate flow and protection in the close proximity of a feed lane or other access to food such as overgrowth overhead. When both conditions are satisfied these places should be best of all.

Not shown, of course, are the majority of areas in rivers which do not satisfy these conditions and where gamefish have no reason to be. These include thin, flat stretches offering little or no concealment and widely scattered food supply; areas with muddy or sandy bottom (without concealment and with less than minimal food supply); and backwaters with little or no current.

In reading water, anglers new to an area should take time before fishing it to study the rocks, edges, runs, feed lanes and deep holes which combine to make up the structure of a river. Spent insects, leaves and other bits of debris drifting downstream mark feed lanes; rocks or other obstructions in these lanes should be noted as possible hot spots. Holding positions inside edges should be noted. "If I were a trout, where would I prefer to be?" is the question to be answered. At first such study takes a bit of time, but the experienced water reader can size up situations at a glance. While you can't catch fish unless your lure is in the water, it pays to devote a few minutes to making the rest of the time more productive.

Since we can't take readers to the river, we'll try to bring interesting spots in several famous rivers to you by analyzing the photographs which follow. It pays to study them. They will be similar to many spots on rivers that you fish.

EDGES FORMED BY PARTIALLY SUBMERGED ROCKS

Looking downstream in this picture, we see a good-looking shale and gravel bottom from which several fairly large rocks emerge. The nearest rock's moderate flow between its edges may be too shallow to interest fish; this depending on the river's height and the amount of protection afforded.

The next rock, to the right, is in much deeper water, with wide edges and a large submerged rock to its right, both combining to make a small feed lane between them. A fairly large trout lies inside the edge in the feed lane, and two others lie in the moderate flow area near the rock's left edge.

Just downstream of this left edge is a small edge made by a submerged rock. The polarized photograph shows a deep hole to the right of this in which a trout is feeding because it is also in the tail of the big edge, the two combining to form a small feeding lane.

Farther downstream, at top left of the picture, a rock forms another wide edge. (The one to the left of it, like the first one we discussed, probably is in water too shallow to be of interest.) A trout lies in the wide right edge, which brings up the point that, when a rock forms two edges, the deeper one nearer midstream usually is the better one.

After fishing these edges we could try another cast or two before moving on. Note that the right edges of the two deepest rocks tend to converge near the spot marked X. This may mean that there is a small, deep channel there, and the combination also indicates a feed lane, so this is a good spot to try. Casts should be swung or drifted upstream of the X and then extended farther downstream.

21

COMPLEX LIES ABOVE AND BELOW STREAM ROCKS

This polarized photograph shows the stream bed quite clearly and brings up a few interesting points.

We note a rather deep riverbed channel flowing in from lower right of the picture between the two lines drawn in to mark it. Several large rocks lie near the middle of the channel just below the center of the picture. The "V" made by the edges of a submerged rock can be seen clearly in the white water below the rock that emerges. A rather indistinct edge is made by the smaller rock at upper right of the emerging one, but the quiet water it forms indicates this.

Just before this picture was taken a fairly large brown trout was hooked between the edges of the white-water "V." Brown trout commonly select a lie behind a rock formation like this. If a rainbow trout was in the area it probably would lie in the faster water of the channel just upstream of the "V," in the protection of this deep stretch, because rainbows usually prefer faster water than brown trout do. If the river contained steelhead during a run, a fish probably would lie in the spot from which the brown trout was taken, or in the deep but protected area of white water near the top right of the picture.

This deep depression, which has been gouged out around the spot marked X at top right, is a good spot for big trout of all species. The flow near the stream bed is moderate because of depth and large rocks there. The lie also is protected by the disturbed surface. An angler would first fish the near channel from a concealed position farther back, paying particular attention to the spot between the legs of the white-water "V." Then he would extend his casts to work his lures through the depression marked X.

A POOL AND RIFFLE WITH INLET STREAM

Under the bridge is a pool which is deep and shaded on its right side at A. This probably isn't a favored spot for trout, but the whole shaded area should be excellent for smallmouth bass. If there are trout there they should be found close to the bank. A cold-water brook runs into the river from the right, at B, and combines with the water of the river to form a visible edge and a deeper channel.

Anglers would fish this stretch by wading out along the riffle from the left bank to thoroughly work the water along the edge. This relatively small area is the best one shown in the picture for trout, but smallmouth bass may be holding near the brook mouth in early morning and late evening, probably moving to the shaded area near the bridge during midday. Absence of rocks in the pool indicates that it should be unproductive for trout, and probably not worth bothering with.

In summer there is another reason why trout may be holding in the area of the edge marked on the picture. Since they shun warm water they may lie in the cooler channel before running up the brook to seek cooler water in small pools. Rainbow trout may run up the brook in spring to spawn, and brown trout and brook trout may do this in the fall. During their spawning runs, trout often lie in rivers (or lakes) near brook mouths, waiting for rain to raise the water and make traveling easier.

FISHING A LARGE EDDY

This is a situation where the right tactics should raise a lunker or two—probably trophy brown trout. Let's sit on a rock, well below the eddy, and try to read what is going on.

The river flows from top right to lower left, riffling down from the pool above. The riffle shelves from the gravel bank at upper left toward the big boulder, which breaks the fast flow of the stream here to make a large, swirling eddy moving in a counterclockwise direction. A pronounced edge extends from the rock's tip downstream just to the left of the long slick caused by the big boulder and subsurface rocks. Other slicks and churning currents indicate more large subsurface rocks, providing excellent holding positions for several trophy-sized fish. Just to the left of the edge the main force of the current is compressed to provide a feed lane, so the fish holding here don't have to travel far for food. The rocks also are sure to harbor schools of minnows.

The trout will probably follow the normal pattern of lying in the moderate flow just inside the edge, but, since the water is rather turbulent, they should be deep, behind subsurface rocks. An upstream cast to the boulder's point, into the foam, allows the lure to run deep, but line must be retrieved rapidly to keep it fairly tight in order to feel strikes. The lure should be fished all the way to the extreme left of the picture, and several casts should be made in order to fish the edge thoroughly.

Casts more inside the edge should then cause the lure to sweep in the counterclockwise direction noted on the photograph. Every attempt should be made to fish the lure deep. Bucktails or streamers on a floating line with a sinking tip, or perhaps weighted nymphs, should help fly fishermen to connect. If weighted lures are used, they should be compact wobblers.

Note that the riffle shelves off deeply around the spot marked X. Fish may be holding in the deep water here just to the right of this spot, perhaps resting in this position preparatory to combatting the fast water of the riffle on their upstream journey. Casts should be made to the upper part of the deep water so the lure will sink and swing down through the "V" of the current and also deeply through the deep-water area.

24

FISHING A DEEP HOLE

Deep holes offer several opportunities for finding fish, and we can assume there are some big ones here. The river is split by a riffle, now out of water, which divides it into the main channel at *A* and a secondary one at *B*, where we notice that it shelves off steeply into the deep hole. We can see the faint edge extending downstream from the rocky point, marked by the line of bits of foam and floating debris. Note that this line curves counterclockwise to form a wide and deep eddy.

Experience tells us that fish can be expected in several positions in a situation like this. There is a deep hole on the other side of the point. Most of the fish will be lying in deep water on the side of the point that is in the shade. During midday on this side of the point they should be hugging bottom, along the edge caused by the point, or under the drop-off at *B*. Lures must dredge bottom.

Probably the best times to fish a deep hole like this are during daybreak and after dusk, when the hole's inhabitants lose some of their caution and roam the pool for food. Then, and particularly when an insect hatch is on, dry flies should furnish good sport, and the lack of conflicting currents indicates that long floats are possible. Lacking a hatch, weighted nymphs should do the trick, because the gravel here should be alive with the naturals. Streamers or bucktails, matched in size, shape and color to prevalent baitfish, should do well, too, particularly when stripped in fairly fast after allowing them to sink deeply. This spot also is a good one for spinners and spoons. If the river contains smallmouth bass, we should find some good ones here.

RIFFLES BELOW AN ISLAND

Islands in moderate or fast-flowing rivers form current edges on their downstream sides. In this situation we have a pointed island in a fast river, producing a distinct edge (1) with the main flow on this side of the island. On the far side of the island is a slow, deep riffle combining with the fast, shallow one on this side. Fish should be lying along the edge on the slow, deep side.

The small outcropping extending into the middle right of the picture causes a secondary edge (2) to flow into the lip of a pool. Fish should be lying in the more moderate flow on the near side of the edge, and the hot spot for them should be just over the lip where the water deepens into the pool.

The nearest edge (3) is probably of minor importance, but darker water on the downstream part of it indicates depth, so it is worth a try even though fish there will probably be smaller. Probability of success is increased because disturbed water in the lower left of the picture indicates there are rocks there which probably rolled down during a freshet.

This is good water for trout, including steelhead, and also for salmon. A hatch of mayflies would tempt us to use dry flies if the water is warmer than 50 degrees, but they must be good floaters.

ERODED RIFFLES AND EDGES

This interesting stretch of river offers several fish-finding clues. At the top of the picture are two eroded gravel riffles (1 and 2) which have been broken down in their centers to form ridges on each side and a short pool or run in between. If the water in the pools or runs is deep enough, and especially if it contains rocks, it may offer good cover for fish. If not, this may be a good feeding area, only a short distance from the protective cover of overgrowth at the top of the picture. During mayfly hatching activity the trout would feed here, usually at dusk, on adult mayflies and nymphs.

Just below the riffle we see the curved edges (3) made by a large submerged rock. If there is a lunker in the pool, this should be his home.

The water in the foreground is relatively shallow, but rocks which have rolled downstream have been deposited at the edge of the faster flow marked by the wavy line (4), where the current deepens. The disturbed surface indicates many subsurface rocks which slow down the flow along the river's bottom here, making this a likely holding and feeding area for trout.

We have seen that gamefish, when not actively feeding on or near the surface, lie in the protective cover of rocks on the bottom in a location like this. We must bounce bottom with our lures, especially when the water is cold. If the lure isn't felt to touch bottom periodically, we aren't fishing deep enough. Getting hung up occasionally and losing a lure or two may be bothersome, but it pays off in more and bigger fish!

A COMPLEX BELOW AN EXPOSED RIFFLE

This riffle, often swept by high water, would offer the same hot spots if it were a permanent island. Of the two channels around it the one on the right is more interesting because of pockets and edges below large rocks there. One of the best ones is marked by a fish symbol, but closer inspection will expose others. We would wade out to the upper part of the riffle and fish down, due to the high bank on the right.

One of the hot spots is where the two currents merge below the riffle. The force of clashing currents gouges out a deep channel here marked by the slick between its edges. This prominent holding and feeding position should be fished thoroughly.

The right edge of this channel merges with the left edge below the exposed rocks, where another deep channel is noted. Since this also is both a feeding and holding position, a big trout or two should be hooked here, too.

To the right of this channel, clearly noted because of its revealing slick, we see a deep hole which is an active eddy. A few good fish should lie in the edge of the eddy, as marked by the symbols.

Just below this, and a partial reason for the eddy, are several large boulders jutting into the stream. The deeper water below them, identified by its darkness, should hold one or more big trout inside the edge. There is a deep run along the steep bank here, with many boulders, edges and pockets. Most of them are holding positions for fish.

To fish the positions it may be possible to wade down between the midstream rocks and the eddy. But if we do this we must be sure of a way out.

A second choice in wading is to cross the white-water riffle between the island and the left bank. Note that the left bank is gradually shelving gravel while the right bank (filled in for a road) is rocky and deeply shelving. Casting may be best from the left bank where one can wade in below the channel formed by the rocks after the position has been fished. Thus it may be possible to cover the rocks on the deeply shelving right side.

A DEEP GLIDE WITH ROCK LEDGES

This position, typical of many rivers, didn't look very interesting until we viewed it with polarized glasses. (The photo was taken with a polarized filter.) Then diagonal pockets between the submerged ledges were revealed in the lower left foreground.

To fish this area successfully we should walk along the road (which skirts the river on the right) to view the water from above, noting the presumed hot spots which can't be seen as clearly from near water level. If we can get down to the river from the road we can probably wade across the riffle below the pool at the top of the picture and fish the long glide from the gravel bank on the left, or by wading the river near that side.

Just below the riffle are many deep holding positions below rocks close to the right bank. Two of the best ones are marked by fish symbols. These can be covered easily. The point to be made here, however, is that dark water indicates a long, deep glide extending downstream between the rock ledges, identified by the lower three fish symbols. This whole glide should be covered thoroughly because it offers both holding and feeding positions. Almost any type of lure could do well here. If fish are not surface feeding, however, we might try streamer flies or bucktails on sinking lines, or spinners or wobblers with spinning tackle, letting the lures run deep.

EDGES AND LIES FORMED BY DEBRIS

We happened to approach these wooded pools when a rise of trout was in progress, and made notes of the actual positions of several of them. By looking carefully, a few of the surface dimples made by rising trout can be seen in the picture. These weren't very big ones, but taking a few on drifting dry flies is what makes angling a cherished sport.

The big tree, which drifted downstream during high water, lodged near the head of this little pool in about three feet of water. Other drifting branches and logs have tangled with it to make an area of moderate flow which is an excellent sanctuary for trout. The edge (1) curving between root and trunk also is a feed lane, and a fly drifted down it should attract the two fish indicated by the symbols. Another feed lane and edge (2) flows beside the main trunk, under which several trout should lie. The object here is to work lures very close to the trunk so they will be in easy reach of fish lying in the shade below it. The other fish indicated by symbols are out in the pools, actively feeding, and haven't been disturbed by the anglers' cautious approach.

Since these pools aren't very deep, artificial flies or nymphs should be better, and offer more sport, than hardware. Dry flies or nymphs are the answer when trout are feeding like this. Drifting nymphs always should be effective in this gravel stream. When no rises are noticed, either nymphs or very small streamers or bucktails, actively stripped in quite deep, should bring strikes.

A LONG POOL WITH SUBMERGED BOULDERS

This pool is similar to others which have been noted; it is a common type distinguished by slowly moving water in which the small edges of submerged rocks are clearly visible. Water in summer is cooled by a fast-flowing inlet stream which enters the pool below the bridge around the river's bend. This is an ideal area for either smallmouth bass or trout.

Some of the probable lies for trout are indicated by symbols, showing that all of the little edges and swirls caused by submerged rocks are good holding spots. Of course the pool would be fished from the left gravel bank toward the right rocky one. It may be better to wade deeply in the pool to keep our silhouette low, working slowly down the pool and handling a fairly long line to disturb the trout as little as possible.

Except for the rocks, all of the pool is fairly fine gravel, which indicates that nymphs, fished slowly, are preferred unless the rises of feeding fish suggest using dry flies. If wobblers or spinners are used they should be small ones, cast to the right bank and allowed to swing in the slight current before being fished in. Small streamers or bucktails in colors simulating prevalent baitfish should also do well when handled in this manner, with added action being imparted by the rod tip. Fly fishermen using submerged attractors should find a floating line with sinking tip and a long, light tapered leader ideal for the purpose.

STEEP BANK WITH OBSTRUCTIONS

In this section of a river in Oregon the steep bank has been eroded over many years by seasonal high water, causing trees to slide down and obstruct the current. Although there are no rocks to make edges and holding water, these situations are formed by other obstructions such as earth slides and fallen trees.

We note quickly that the near side of the stream is slowly shelving and wadable, while the far one is very deep. Anglers fishing this stretch wade the near side and cast to pockets and into edges formed by obstructions such as the dead tree at right and the trunk extending into the water at left. These obstructions produce a distinct edge on the far side, providing moderate flow for holding water, plus concealment. We also note by the foam line that a nearer edge, extending down to the angler, is caused by the slowly shelving water behind the angler being gouged out deeply in front of him by the force of the current. He is standing at the edge of the drop-off.

Lures should be fished deep inside the edges behind obstructions. With fly rods, sinking lines should be used with streamers or bucktails, or steelhead flies when runs are going upstream. At other times anglers fish for big brown trout or rainbows. Surface feeding would recommend buoyant dry flies—Wulff patterns or an Irresistible, for example.

SHALLOW RUN AND ROCK-FILLED RIFFLE

This photo shows a flat, shallow run flowing into a short, rock-filled midstream riffle. When the picture was taken rainbow trout were feeding on emerging mayfly nymphs, their positions marked here by symbols.

Here, the edge is indistinct, but one is caused by midstream rocks and is noted primarily by a faint foam line which also is the most pronounced feed lane nearby. The feeding trout are just inside of this. Others may be feeding near the lip of the run (to the left of the angler's shoulder), but this isn't as good a spot, mainly because it lacks good feed lanes.

While the angler was fly fishing with nymphs here we noted other rainbows feeding in the moderate flow near the far bank. There is an edge of a current line there which can't be seen in the picture.

This photograph was taken by Bud Lilly, famous angler and tackle shop owner of West Yellowstone, Montana. The angler is equally famous photographer and angling author Rex Gerlach. Note his wading staff, prudently carried for use in deep, fast stretches. The area around West Yellowstone contains several of America's finest trout rivers.

A DEEP, ROCK-FILLED RUN

One of America's most fascinating and productive trout rivers is the famous Firehole in the Yellowstone area. Geysers and hot springs (as shown here) warm the cold water to temperatures ideal for trout, while the introduced mineral content encourages mosses and grasses which are copious breeding grounds for aquatic foods of all sorts.

The picture shows a deep, rock-filled run which might reveal no distinguishing characteristics to the casual angler unskilled in reading the water. Closer inspection shows a few trouty hot spots. The most prominent of these is the underwater rock mass at the left of the picture which forms wide edges and a moderate flow area between them. This is excellent brown trout water, and a good one measuring twenty-six inches was taken here on a dry fly just before this picture was taken.

Another feature is the rather indistinct edge, also formed by rocks, extending downstream to the left of the angler. The force of the current is directed by these into a channel between the two edges. This provides a glide of moderate flow along the right bank extending down to the hot spring. Anglers habitually use hard-to-sink dry flies on these rivers and take pride in releasing most of the trout they catch. The practice of "catch and release" allows trophy fish to be hooked several times, providing better sport for anglers and assuring maximum propagation of trout.

A WEEDY MEADOW STRETCH

We just noted that lime and other minerals dissolved in the waters of several rivers in the Yellowstone area and elsewhere encourage dense growths of weeds which are nurseries for food for trout. This river, the Firehole, in the Yellowstone area flows through a meadow stretch containing grassy islands. A fairly level gravel bottom contains many hummocks from which sprout weeds that extend to lie on the surface.

This photograph, by Bud Lilly, shows such a stretch, but the weedy patches are hard to see in it. An island juts downstream in the middle of the picture. Large edges extend downstream from both sides, as marked. Fish lie inside the edges of this relatively weedless area and, since insect hatches occur very often in season, selected trout are easy to locate. The locations are marked of several which were seen rising when this picture was taken. Note the hole occupied by the one at the left. The angler hooked the fish shown on a nymph at the very point of the island.

STEELHEAD RIVERS

Being an easterner, I have fished for Atlantic salmon more than I have for sea-run rainbow trout, whose stamina and exceptional fighting ability have earned them the name of "steelhead." On western angling trips to fabled rivers such as the Deschutes and the Klamath, I have noted a great similarity between the habits of Atlantic salmon and steelhead. Much of what follows, then, also applies to Atlantic salmon, and to Pacific salmon as well.

To conserve energy, all anadromous fish in fast water select the easiest way to ascend the river—the path of moderate flow, even if it runs close to shore. These fish also rest in water of moderate flow, such as between the current edges behind rocks, along ledges, or in the depths of cold-water pools. When an impediment to their passage is reached, such as a stretch of long, rough rapids or a waterfall, many of the fish will hold in the first major moderate-flow area below this point, either to regain strength before going up, or to wait for higher water which would make the passage easier.

Another fact to consider: Since these fish have spent long periods in the ocean where man has not bothered them to any extent, their fear of people is minimal. Unlike skittish freshwater species such as trout, anadromous fish seldom seek hiding places and often lie in plain sight in shallow pools and other holding positions. Their fear of man is so slight that a wading angler must almost shove them to make them move. This is unfortunate because it makes them easy prey for poachers.

Atlantic salmon can be taken legally only with artificial flies, but they would strike at other lures if they were offered. Other lures and baits are used for steelhead, particularly in the winter, but the greatest sport is to seek them with artificial flies in warmer weather.

Let's study a few typical situations:

A CLASSIC BOULDER-FILLED RUN

This photograph is of the legendary Estuary Drift on Washington's Grand Ronde River, once one of the world's greatest steelhead fishing drifts. During peak migration periods as many as forty fish were hooked here in a day.

The river here drops into the run from rapids a quarter of a mile long, offering tempting holding places. The configuration of the drift, marked on the picture, can easily be seen. At this edge the depth averages about five feet, with a current speed of about six miles per hour at the upper part of the run slowing to about four miles per hour in the unseen pool to the left.

The bottom of this typical holding water is strewn with large rocks and boulders, none of which extend above the surface and all of which contribute to moderate flow. This entire stretch is such an excellent holding area that steelhead could be hooked anywhere in the drift. In the Northeast such a spot would be equally good for Atlantic salmon.

A JOINING OF CURRENTS

We now know that where two currents join, such as below an island or where a stream enters a river, an edge is formed in which fish may lie on the side offering moderate flow or agreeable temperature. The edge shown here (1) is such a place, and the hot spot is at A because the joining currents have formed a deep, boulder-filled run there.

Note also the current line in the foreground. This stretch of deeper and more moderate flow offers fish an easier travel route up through the rapids coming in at the left. The current edge is inside line 2, which is an established path of migration upstream. Fish are hooked consistently in the locations indicated by the symbols. This particular drift has been one of the most consistently productive stretches of water in the Northwest.

LEDGEROCK HOLDING WATER

Another classic holding position for steelhead is very close to a bedrock ledge, either in a pool or, as in this case, immediately upstream from a powerful rapids. If the face of the rock ledge is at an angle down current, as this one is, an edge is formed to provide moderate flow. Lies like this always are good because when a fish is taken from one another fish will move in to occupy it. Anglers should remember such places, and mark their locations in a notebook.

I have in mind such a ledge in a favorite pool on Quebec's Matapedia River. Although its face points diagonally upstream, it is in a tiny and over-grown cove of the shore which causes a slight eddy in water about two feet deep. The spot doesn't seem to go by the rules unless one examines it closely, and I found it only because a gust of wind directed the fly off course. It happened to drop in the eddy close to the ledge. A tremendous boil of water erupted there, and I was fast to a big salmon. On a trip down the pool two days later I took another one there, and nearly always have connected on other trips since then. It must be an ideal lie because a salmon in the twenty-five-pound class or bigger usually occupies it. Salmon and steelhead rivers often are changed by freshets, sometimes wiping out valuable pools while forming others, and eliminating good holding positions while scouring out new ones. Such changes are uncommon in permanent ledgerock, so good positions usually remain so year after year.

A CLASSIC LEDGEROCK TRAVEL ROUTE

Here, a ledge which can be seen entering the river on the far bank extends across the river to turn the upstream rapids into a fairly deep pool. Steelhead habitually go upstream along the far bank and cross in the protection of the ledge to swim the rapids along the deeper and slower right-hand side. When fish are on the move in overcast weather, or between late afternoon and mid-morning, lures fished close to the ledge often enough should bring frequent strikes.

Since we are trying for moving fish here, rather than resting ones, the lure and a moving fish must be in the same place at the same time. Sooner or later, however, the angler who keeps his fly or lure in the water can be sure a fish swimming through the run will see it.

Steelhead, like other anadromous salmonoids, follow the same age-old travel routes year after year during upstream migrations. Although these travel routes may change somewhat from year to year in streams with gravel or sandy bottoms, due to the scouring of the stream sides during high water, ledges formed by bedrock remain constant, at least during an angler's lifetime. Since the deep water protected by the ledge has moderate flow this also may be a good holding position for several fish regaining their strength preparatory to the trip up the rapids.

HOLDING POSITIONS IN RAPIDS

This spot, similar to some of the examples of holding positions for trout, is typical for steelhead also. The polarized photograph shows several deep pockets behind large boulders offering potential resting lies. Positions A and B seem the best ones because several big rocks provide edges between which the stream bottom has been scoured out deeply. Other good locations are indicated by fish symbols.

Water like this can be fished most effectively with large, colorful steelhead hairwing wet flies on a floating line or a floating line with a sinking tip. Casts should be made quartering down and across stream, first working the fly along the current edges below the rocks and then, on later casts, making it sweep directly through the pockets themselves. When the fly has completed its swing, let it hang downstream and work it actively before fishing it in. Steelhead often follow a fly but may not take it until its action changes.

Polarized sunglasses are a necessity for reading water properly. They cut down or eliminate glare, allowing us to see below the surface. Here they help us to locate the pockets, determine their depth and see the fish.

HOLDING WATER IN A DEEP POOL

Steelhead do most of their upstream traveling on cloudy, overcast days and during the night. On bright days they frequently will be holding in deep pools wherever obstructions provide edges, or beside steep banks. This example of a large boulder, which could be a protruding bedrock ledge, offers a perfect example of a likely pool lie. If the day is bright it may be most effective to present the fly deeply on a fast-sinking or sinking-tip line. On an overcast day a lightly dressed fly could be drifted into the position to coax the fish into a rising take.

Good steelhead lies in pools don't always depend on obstructions which provide moderate flow. Shallow depressions in the stream bed—small dished-out areas of bathtub size or smaller—create pockets of moderate flow under the fast-flowing current. Such unconcealed depressions may be occupied by other species of anadromous fish. I have often seen Atlantic salmon holding in such spots, sometimes near the tails of pools where the water otherwise is too shallow to accommodate them. They may do this in bright sunlight in gravel areas where they are easily visible.

HOLDING WATER IN A DEEP RUN

This run appears shallow because the photo was taken with a polarized lens. Actually, it is about six feet deep. When large boulders are in a run (even a fast one) the chances are good that they will shelter holding fish.

The trick here is to get the fly or lure down deep because the fish lie close to the bottom. The combination of a weighted fly and an extra-fast-sinking line, with the cast made well above the position, should do it, working the deeply sunken fly as close as possible to the edge.

If spinners or wobblers are used they should be compact and fast-sinking. Cast them up and across current and work them close to the bottom near the boulders.

In bottom dredging there is an axiom that if you don't lose a lure or get hung up occasionally, you're not fishing deep enough. Summer steelhead are more active than winter steelhead, and will move farther for the fly or lure. The cold water makes winter steelhead almost dormant, so they hug bottom and won't move very far to take a lure or bait. Baits are very popular for winter-run fish; usually salmon eggs or salmon-egg clusters. Experts roll and bounce these along the bottom and can feel them ticking bottom as they are carried downstream. Pencil leads on light droppers that break loose when stuck are necessary when bottom-bouncing for winter steelhead.

HOLDING WATER AT THE TOP OF A RAPIDS

This is a ledgerock run at the upstream end of a long rapids. After resting to regain their strength in the moderate flow of pools or runs below, the fish nearly exhaust themselves by fighting the long, fast current while picking their way between the rocks of the rapids to reach the upper end. Many of them become so tired they stop in any sanctuary they can find. Thus, they will rest behind rocks near the top of a rapids in water that may seem too fast for them.

Since such sanctuaries are more or less marginal, a fish won't hold here long, preferring a position of more moderate flow farther up when it has regained enough strength to reach it. During a run, however, new fish will stop in such positions after others have vacated them, so holding positions in this fast water may be continuously occupied.

This type of water offers a classic example of where to find resting sea-run rainbow trout near the top of a rapids when migrations of the fish are in progress.

A TRAVEL ROUTE THROUGH A DEEP POOL

Steelhead are noted for traveling near the edge of the main current flow, almost never in the stronger current, and often very close to shore because deeper and more moderate current may be there. The ideal current speed for a steelhead run is about five miles per hour, as fast as a man can walk briskly. Ideal depth for fly fishing is between three and five feet. This classic pool contains all the requirements.

Note that the main current through the pool is on the left-hand side, leaving a fairly deep area of more moderate flow near the bank on the right. The usual path of migration through this pool is noted by the dashed line, with symbols denoting fish along it. We also note submerged rocks and their edges near the upstream end. Fish may be holding in these positions, and others may be passing them.

This pool should be fished from the right side if the water there can be waded or if casts can be made from the bank. We would first cover the visible holding positions, then let the fly or lure swing deeply along the presumed path of migration as we fish down the pool. Casts should be made directly to the left bank to give the fly or lure time to sink deeply.

A TRAVEL ROUTE UP A CLASSIC GLIDE

By now we should be able to read this glide merely by glancing at it. The current on the near side is deeper and more moderate than on the far side, with a definite edge, indicated by the dashed line, separating the two. Steelhead traveling routes such as this normally go up close to the outside edge of the main thrust of the current, as noted by the symbols. Large boulders, indicated by the slicks, may hold fish.

This glide would be fished by wading down the left side of the river if casts to the right bank can be made from there. In such an exposed area fishing should be best on a bright day early in the morning or after dusk. On overcast days it may be good around noon. Of course lures must be fished deep, and we should feel them making contact with rocks on the bottom.

FISH THE SHADY SIDE

Let's end this chapter with an important lesson. This photograph, by Bob Candy, of Vermont's Fish and Game Department, shows a stretch of the famous Battenkill River, one of my favorite trout streams. The angler is drifting a dry fly down the run close to the far bank. The point I want to make is that, when other conditions are compatible, it is better to fish the shady side of a stream than the sunny side. Trout will travel far to seek shade because it offers comfort and concealment.

Here, big trees and smaller bushes overhang the shady side, so terrestrial insects and other foods will drop in the water. The water is deep and of moderate flow. The bank is probably undercut. The place has all the earmarks of a hot spot.

3

Finding Fish
in Streams and Brooks

While many anglers prefer the challenges of big rivers and the bigger fish usually found in them, at least as many seek the fascinating mysteries of smaller streams and brooks. Trout fishing in America had its genesis in small waters—Theodore Gordon's favorite Willowemoc and the fabled Beaverkill into which it flows. This area, in New York's Catskill Mountains, is revered as the cradle of American trout fishing and was the mecca for famous anglers at the turn of the century.

Many of us prefer the challenges of smaller waters; they are ever-changing, testing an angler's skill and strategy at every bend. Big trout lurk in protected areas down their courses, but if you disturb the surface with poor casts, or show yourself, or make noise, you never see them except as fleeing shadows. The choice of fly is important, but even more so is proper presentation and knowing *where* to cast. That is what this chapter is about.

A POOL BELOW A WATERFALL

Small dams and waterfalls fascinate anglers, particularly those new at the game, partly because of their beauty but mainly because they think the well-aerated depths beneath them hold the biggest lunkers in the stream. Even if this is so, chances are that the big ones spend daylight hours in unreachable recesses behind the waterfall and only venture into the pool itself late in the day or at night in search of food.

This picture shows a natural dam made by large boulders in the rapids from which the stream cascades into a small pool with numerous deep pockets caused by other rocks below. If we can sneak up behind the boulder at lower right and flick a fly into the little pocket at the top of the edge, we could get an immediate strike from a good fish lying inside the edge near the base of the main waterfall at left. The edge of white water beside a small cascade such as this is an ideal lie for a feeding trout.

The fly would then drift down along the edge to tempt a trout in the deep pocket in the foreground. Other short casts should be made to the pocket under the overhanging rock at left and into the little edge made by the smaller cascade in the middle of the picture. A weighted nymph or a lively worm with a split-shot or two about six inches above it should be fished close to the pool's bottom. In clement weather, and particularly when the pool is in shade, feeding trout should hit lures solidly and instantly. The fast water doesn't allow them much time to make a decision!

A WELL-SHADED POOL

Spots like this are favorite lairs for big trout as well as problems for anglers. At the base of the "U" formed by the gravel bar we should assume that the stream, flowing over the riffle at upper right, undercuts the bank below the bushes at left to form a deep and well-protected channel.

In meadow streams these U-turns usually gouge out the bank on the outside of the "U" to form a deep channel which can be an ideal lie for trout. The situation is even better here because the overhanging bushes provide shade as well as insects, caterpillars and other foods which drop down from them. The ideal time to fish places like this is when the pool is in shadow. Of course the fish lie well back under the bushes, which is part of the problem.

Not knowing what the foreground approach offers, the best way for the angler to work into position is to creep across the gravel bar to partial concealment behind one of the tree stumps. A patient angler would wriggle flat on his stomach! Raising his rod only high enough to make a horizontal cast, he would try to put the lure well under the bushes, as far upstream as possible, so it would drift under the overhang. If the lure isn't a natural bait it should be an imitation of a grub, a grasshopper, a jassid or some other natural food of the season. The strongest sensible tippet should be used because entanglement in the bush is probable. If the hooked fish jumps, all one can do is pull and pray!

A RIFFLE AND POOL COMBINATION

This beautiful S-shaped stretch shows an upper pool (A) and a lower pool (B) divided by a short riffle. The upper pool, nearly always in shade, is about four feet deep and contains a six-foot hole behind a large boulder. Fish roam it more or less freely in search of food.

Since the lower pool is exposed to sun during midday it should be fished in early morning or around dusk when no sunlight strikes the surface. The best approach to both is by wading downstream with as low a profile as possible.

The lower pool is about six feet deep in the center of the channel (below the edge) but doesn't appear so because the photo was taken with a polarized filter to reveal large, submerged boulders there. Remember that there are edges around submerged rocks as well as emerging ones, and that they should be fished thoroughly as has been described.

Ordinarily, and especially when light is on the pool, the fish lie behind the protection of rocks fairly close to the edge. One therefore directs casts to the near bank to let submerged flies or lures swing toward the edge, or he drifts dry flies down inside the edge where the fish symbols are shown.

A wide choice of lures is appropriate for such a long, deep pool. Small spinners or wobblers would do well when worked deep. So would small streamers or bucktails, nymphs, dry flies "matching the hatch," or representations of grasshoppers or grubs. Note what is crawling or flying, and try to imitate it.

A POOL UNDER A ROCK FACE

The current here flows in over the riffle at the left, forcefully strikes the ledge and is diverted downstream to the right. Note that the gravel bank in the foreground extends halfway across the stream, where it drops steeply because the current has gouged it out there. The deep water along the cliff face provides excellent lies for some of the biggest fish in the stream.

After striking the ledge, part of the current is forced into a large eddy (A). The downstream edge of this eddy is a good lie for a big trout. The rest of the current joins that from the eddy to form a smooth pool at B which is about eight feet deep. One or more big trout should inhabit this pool, probably very close to the rock. The cliff face is in deep shadow except for a short time at midday, thus giving the fish a sense of security.

Except when insects are hatching and fish are seen to be taking them on the surface we probably will have to work lures very deep to have them taken in this eddy and pool. Of course this is a good bait hole if one wishes to use lead to get the bait down. Weighted spinners may do the trick, but a small, compact heavy wobbling spoon such as a Wob-L-Rite should do better. Fly fishermen would choose a weighted nymph on a fast-sinking line. The current will take lures into position, but casts should be made to the cliff face, well to the left of the picture.

THE TAIL OF A LONG GRAVEL POOL

This is the end of a long pool with a gravel bottom containing scattered rocks. It empties into a wide riffle which flows into another pool below. The tail of the pool is deeper than one would expect, ranging to almost three feet below the submerged rock in the lower foreground. Trout in this pool usually feed on nymphs which cling to rocks on the bottom; otherwise, the fish take the hatching insects on top.

In a gravel pool, most of the trout will be in different positions when they are resting than when they are feeding. Resting positions are indicated by the fish symbols. In the right foreground several rocks make edges which are good lies for fish, as indicated. Other unseen submerged rocks nearer the tail of the pool also may harbor resting fish, and they may be seen rising and feeding from these positions from time to time.

During other periods and especially when major insect hatches occur, usually near dusk in warm weather, feeding trout may drop to the tail of the pool and look for food near the major feed lanes.

There are three major current tongues leaving the pool—one near each bank and one in the middle. Trout on the feed will usually lie in moderate current near the tongues, or feed lanes, and dash out into the faster water from time to time to snatch drifting food. Probable positions are noted with X's.

The best way to fish this pool would be to work upstream using dry flies or nymphs. Spinners such as the C. P. Swing and the Mepps should also produce. Cast them out and let them swing on a tight line to cover rocks and current lanes.

STREAM BED DEPRESSIONS

This is a familiar situation, a pool emptying over a riffle into a deep depression in the stream bed. Viewed in unfiltered light this run wouldn't look productive, but it was photographed with a polarized lens to show the depression and the current edge.

Note that large, submerged boulders, particularly near the lower end of the depression, provide excellent cover for trout. The current edge is clearly marked, but the important edges are caused by rocks on the bottom. The water above the current edge is shallow and worthless.

In season this stretch should be interesting dry-fly water, and the fish should respond to nymphs. Small streamers or bucktails worked around the edges of rocks should produce. Spinners would do better here than wobblers because deep-running lures aren't necessary. Dry flies or nymphs should be allowed to follow the current lane. Streamers, bucktails and metal lures can be cast quartering downstream and across and allowed to work edges behind the rocks. Casting can be done from either side but it would be better to start at the base of the riffle on the far side and to fish down the channel.

UNDERCUT RIVER BANKS

Here is an interesting meadow stretch where the current veers to the left and erodes the bank. Note that all of the thick turf in the middle of the picture has been undercut and has fallen into the stream. When this happens large slabs of the peaty turf hold together to provide small caves and tunnels under the fallen bank through which part of the stream flows. The banks abound with grasshoppers and grubs, which often drop into the stream; also, large numbers of hatched aquatic insects fall or are blown onto the currents below.

This is an excellent location for trophy brown trout, which lie protected in the coves, edges and tunnels, always ready to dash from cover to snatch food.

The water on this side of the stream's edge holds no promise, so the idea is to work lures as close to the left bank as possible. The obstruction at far left provides an edge and a deep hole which should harbor a big trout. So does the grassy hummock just below it, as well as the branch jutting into the stream.

I would select a fluffy marabou streamer fly of average size and would fish it upward and downward as close to the bank as possible to provide maximum pulsating action. Why? Because marabou streamers are attractive to big brown trout, especially when they are made to pulsate in one position for a minute or two. Perhaps they look like an enticing new form of food, but they also may incite a big trout to strike out of anger. A light marabou like the Ballou Special is a good choice for a bright day in clear water, but a brown or black one is preferable on an overcast day.

A TRICKY SPOT BELOW BOULDERS

Streams flowing through forested land often present tricky casting problems where downed timber and bushes make accurate lure delivery almost impossible. Casual anglers will glance at such a place and leave it for stretches that are easier. More serious ones will wade downstream slowly and quietly, studying the opportunities, and end up with more trout.

It pays to study the shady edges because trout will lie and feed close to them. It pays to drop a fly or bait into rock-made pockets such as the one in left foreground. We noticed three fair-sized trout lying here; one in the left pocket, one in the little pool beside its right edge, and the biggest of all in the deep pocket beneath the boulder at the place marked A. This trout was hooked by floating a fly downstream, but it snagged the leader on a broken branch of the fallen pine and broke away.

In addition to edges, pockets, holes and undercut banks, look for sunken masses of dead leaves in the shade. The careful observer may see several trout lying over them, nearly indistinguishable because of their protective coloration.

AN UNDERWATER LEDGE IN A POOL

This pool doesn't have clearly defined edges since there are no large rocks to break the current. The trout seek protection and shade by the submerged steps of the ledge, several of which can be seen. If any provide overhangs in moderate to deep water, they would be the best lies.

The water close to the ledge offers moderate flow. If you look closely at the V-shaped niche marked *A*, you can see a trout lying over the upper submerged step. When this picture was taken three other trout were seen close to the ledge. Probably the cliff gives the trout a sense of security. Their protective coloration blends with the walls of the underwater steps.

Of course we would fish this location from the near side, trying to drift a dry fly or nymph with the current as close to the walls of the ledge as possible. When a hatch of flies is on, feeding trout should be cruising freely about the pool, retreating when necessary to the sheltering shade of the ledge.

A SHORELINE RUN BESIDE A LEDGE

The camera's polarized lens allows us to see as deeply into this run as we could view it with polarized glasses. Look closely to see a twelve-inch trout lying on feeding station in the little depression at A. Another trout (which can't be seen) was observed lying in the upstream end of the deep pocket at B.

Note that centuries of current erosion have deeply undercut this ledge. Trout can find sanctuary beneath it. There may have been as many as a dozen good-sized ones in this stretch. There is a complexity of current edges, one behind every substantial outcropping, and these as well as the deep pockets provide resting places for fish. The trout venture from these during a hatch to feed on insects, but there is minor need for this because the supply of nymphs is abundant and the feeding lane passes close beside protective outcroppings and over pockets near the ledge.

A hard-to-sink dry fly, such as a Wulff pattern, should do well here, but a weighted nymph may be even better. Fishermen with spinning tackle could sneak to the top of the run and work a small spinner or wobbling spoon through it.

CURRENT EDGES CAUSED BY A ROCK LEDGE

This photograph shows rapids on a small stream breaking over a rock ledge into a pool below. The principal current edges are indicated. Since the main current edge also is the most prominent feed lane, we can confidently presume that large trout are lying near the edge, such as in positions *A*, *B* and *C*. Probably one of the biggest lies in the protected eddy at *D*.

This is the edge to fish first rather than spooking the larger trout by casting to other spots. Then we would cast to *X* close to the upstream side of the tree trunk. The hole below the midstream rocks also looks good. After covering the pool's inlet in this manner we would look for other trouty spots in the pool itself.

AN EDGE CAUSED BY A TREE TRUNK

The peculiar position of this tree trunk illustrates that a log or trunk root system at any angle in a fast stream forms an important edge. In this case the feed lane from above merges with the edge to provide a protected feeding station of moderate flow which could be occupied by several fish. When not actively feeding the fish may be resting under the overhanging rocks at position A. This combination of nearby feeding and resting water is almost sure to harbor one or more large trout, so we look for such places and fish them carefully.

We would approach cautiously from above the right side of the picture, where a high weed growth would partially conceal us. A sinking lure should be cast well upstream of the tree trunk to provide a deep drift down through the feed lane. A floating fly could be dropped in the lane closer to the trunk.

Since this is a gravel stretch a slightly weighted nymph is a good choice. Some fishermen have poor results with weighted nymphs because they are overweighted, causing them to travel too fast and unnaturally. More moderate weighting, with one-ampere fuse wire, allows them to sink slowly and to move more naturally.

A HOLDING SPOT IN AN EDDY

Active eddies are often preferred holding and feeding positions for trout. A three-pound brook trout lives in this one, having been caught and returned to the water at least twice. Here the current momentarily swirls between the rock face itself and a large part of it which broke off to produce the eddy. The big trout can lie in the moderate flow of one or more crevices here and select foods swirled in to him. Probably he rarely ventures from this hiding hole except at dusk or during the night, when he scours the pool for baitfish, nymphs, crayfish or whatever else takes his fancy.

The current, pouring in from the left, widens its edges upon entering the pool. The pool holds smaller trout, some of which lie in the protection of submerged rocks in the area of moderate flow marked X. The weeds and bushes in the left foreground offer partial concealment for anglers who approach this hot spot cautiously.

MULTIPLE SHORELINE EDDIES AGAINST A ROCK FACE

On happening upon a spot like this, anglers who can read the water should hook some of the largest trout in the stream. Others who are less skilled probably would direct casts nearer to the middle of the pool and miss its several hot spots.

The current from the short riffle at the left washes food directly against the rock face. The current eddies into each of the rocky niches, causing floating or submerged foods to hesitate and swirl for several seconds before continuing along the edge downstream. Trout should lie in the crevices of each of the eddies.

The approach here would be from the left shoreline, keeping as low as possible. There is a good holding position below where water breaks over the boulder at the spot marked X, but the canny angler probably would work his lure through this place after casting into or slightly above the large eddy at the left. We would fish each eddy down the rock face in turn, casting a bit above it and as close to the ledge as possible.

A DEEP ROCKY RUN

Deep rocky runs in mountain streams like this are common all the way from the Northwest to New England. The trout in this easy-to-read run lie close to the stream's edges, as indicated. The one on the left enjoys obvious protection in the hole inside the little edge provided by the boulder. Other fish may lie anywhere in the moderate-flow side of the edge running down the middle of the pool because the bottom offers the protection of many large boulders. Another good spot should be under the overhanging rock at the middle of the right side of the picture. The stream's edges and the best of the rocky protection offered tell the story.

These are feeding positions and may also be resting spots. When not actually feeding, the trout should be cruising about near the bottom of the deep eddying pool at the right center of the picture.

This excellent trout water is ideal for fishing a weighted nymph or a small spinner or wobbler. We would cautiously approach the run by climbing over the rocks from upstream. Nymphs should be drifted down the edges of the current, but hardware can be cast to the far bank and allowed to swing to the near one, or can be fished down the current and then slowly retrieved.

A POCKET IN THE RAPIDS

Fast rocky streams may look discouraging to anglers unfamiliar with them. Where could trout lie and feed with ease and security? In addition to occasional pools, search for pockets behind midstream rocks or against a bank.

Here's an interesting pocket of the latter type. A big trout always claims it, driving smaller inhabitants somewhere else. The one holding here when this picture was taken only had to move a few inches to help himself to foods washed his way by the sparkling clear current.

Since stoneflies are abundant in this northwestern stream, the best lure is an artificial stonefly nymph. A cast to the upper edge of the white water nearest the pocket should take the fly into position for an immediate strike.

A STREAM-BED HOLE

When mountain streams have descended nearly to meadow areas they become less turbulent, easier to read—and to fish. This stream-bed depression is more than a pocket, because water flowing over ledgerock or a row of flat boulders has formed a deep hole which is sure to contain trout. We also note a few small pockets with their slightly streaming edges along the tilted outcropping on the far side. We know that such sanctuaries probably contain trout, too.

This spot should be approached from above, and the bait or fly allowed to wash into the hole on a slack line. Several casts can be made from above to thoroughly explore the hole and to probe its length. If small spinners or wobblers are used, try the same tactic or cast to the ledge to swing them into the depression. Small lures are preferable, for trout in this narrow stream may not be very big.

Sinking lures, including small streamers and bucktails, can first be cast to the small pockets along the outcropping and then be allowed to swing and dart into the hole. Tiny bucktails not over an inch or so long, sparsely dressed and with silver tinsel bodies, are good for this if the water contains baitfish.

EDGES BELOW BRIDGES

Edges made by bridge supports usually harbor numerous trout. Fish also hug the supports under the bridge because shade and a bit of more moderate flow are found there. When this picture was taken a large rainbow trout was seen just inside the edge. Smaller fish were spotted as noted.

We see that these fish are lying in the shade supplied by the bridge. The spot would produce little or nothing when it is in the sun. Around dusk the fish would leave the bridge supports to roam the pool; then dry flies, nymphs or small bucktails would produce. If possible, we would wade downstream from above the bridge so lures could swing close to the supports. The hot spot is probably at the upper end of the edge close to the support when this area is in shade.

In New England, at least, hatchery trucks do much of their stocking the easy way by releasing fish from bridges or close beside them. Greedy fishermen start in as soon as a truck leaves and easily deplete many of the fish. Since they are used to being fed, these tame trout are too easy to catch, and not very good to eat. Presumably the fishermen who do this think that the fee they pay for licenses entitles them to whatever they can get. No skill is involved and it would be much better if people would let the tame trout alone, at least until they become acclimated to their surroundings and have taken possession of their fighting instincts.

The currents near the center of this pool indicate the presence of submerged rocks. These should be good lies for trout, and the pool also should harbor smallmouth bass. Smallmouths take the same flies and lures that trout do and roam pools freely even when sun is on them.

AN "S" BEND IN A MEADOW STREAM

Unlike mountain streams, meadow streams are rarely rocky; sometimes the bottoms are gravel but usually they're sandy or muddy. These streams may wriggle in such complex curves that a mile of stream occupies only a small area. Favorite places for trout are at the curves, where banks are often undercut and where the flow digs deeply into the outside of the curve to provide the safety of depth and the scoured exposure of food-bearing gravel.

The meadow stream shown here is typical, but often the banks are grassy rather than bushy. Anglers would approach each curve stealthily, often on hands and knees, because the trout are exposed and therefore shy.

In this picture the stream flow enters from lower left, fans out into a deep pool at *A;* swings against the undercut shore at *B*, and undercuts again

around the bend at *C*. Probably there are trout in the deep pool marked *A* and, as indicated, there should be several lying below the undercut banks at *B* and *C*.

Let's look at the situation at bend *C*, which is typical of a sharp bend in a meadow stream. The illustration shows that the current, forced into a semicircle, applies its centrifugal power to the outside of the bend to scour the bank and stream bottom deeply there and often to undercut it so that big slabs of turf have fallen into the stream. In most cases the outside bank provides depth and protection, with the principal feed lane close to it. The opposite bank is a sandy or muddy shelf, and of no interest to fish.

If we approach places like this from the shelving bank we will probably be seen. The trick is to sneak to the upstream edge of the curve and to fish it from there as well concealed as possible. Banks like these act as sounding boards, echoing noises into the water, so a quiet approach is essential. Even another angler walking the bank at some distance can scare the trout at our position and ruin the fishing.

Since all of the brook flows moderately, edges, if any, can be unimportant, but those offering depth and concealment should be explored. These often are caused by logs, turf masses and deep indentations in the bank. A brook entering the stream usually scours a deep hole there which can be a hot spot, particularly if it is well shaded. In pastureland, where one property abuts another, we may find an uncleared section of trees or dense bushes, perhaps so entangled that other anglers walk around it. It often pays to get into the brook and to fish the spot.

UNDERCUTS AND A SIDE CHANNEL

Here the stream divides almost equally into side channels, rejoining about a hundred yards downstream to the right. Undercuts at points *A* and *B* are excellent trout lies but the unstable footing in the marshy meadow complicates the approach, which must be made by crawling.

At this point the stream channel is too deep to wade. Presentation of the fly to lie *A* must be made from upstream at *C*. A slack-line downstream offering is preferable in the case of lie *B*, made well back from the bank at location *D*.

A side channel leaves the stream at *E* where turf clumps made a small eddy and a deep pocket. When a hatch occurs the floating duns drift on the eddying current into the pocket and the trout come out from under the grassy banks to feed upon them actively.

BEAVER PONDS

Many streams are dammed by beavers, but the ponds don't always contain trout. We can divide them into two classes. Some, mainly in flat meadows, are more or less stagnant, with insufficient flow to cool the water, and with rotting vegetation caused by water spreading over land areas. A telltale sign of these is the bubbles of marsh gas rising from the muddy bottom due to decomposition. The water lacks sufficient oxygen and it is too warm for trout. The other kinds of interest to anglers are ponds created by beavers in flowing streams, usually in hilly country. The current of the cold-water brook keeps the pond cool and properly oxygenated, carrying away contamination of rotting vegetation, which usually is minimal in such places. Trout seek, and thrive in, little ponds like this because they prefer their moderate flow to the faster water of the brooks and because surrounding vegetation provides both food and shade. A pond of this type is shown in the photo. Typical trout lies are marked, but there are others.

One would approach a pond like this from below the dam, using whatever concealment it affords. If no surface feeding is noted, the trick is to use horizontal casts to drop lures as close under the bushes as possible. After that, look the place over for deep, dark holes. Trout may be concentrated in them. Look for evidence of springs trickling in or coming up from the bottom. The best spot of all may be where the stream enters the pond.

SMALL MEADOW BROOKS

One of my friends enjoys the challenge of meadow brooks so small that he can step across in many places. Several years ago he took me to one, asked me to set up dry-fly tackle with a short leader, and handed me a clipped deer-hair imitation of a bee that he had originated for this kind of fishing. The brook seemed to be no more than a ditch, so small that casting into it would be difficult. Needing instruction and lacking enthusiasm, I lagged behind to watch him.

He dropped to hands and knees at some distance from the brook and wriggled forward as a cat might stalk a mouse. Near the bank he made a short cast, the fly landing on a blade of grass within inches of the water. With a slight twitch he pulled it in—and got an immediate strike from a bright ten-inch brook trout, which he promptly hoisted onto the bank.

Now full of interest at this astonishing trick, I crept to the brook and looked in. Both sides were deeply undercut; the water was cool and deep, with only a narrow band of sunlight to break the shade.

"Almost no one bothers with brooks like this," said my friend, "because they don't look like much. Those that do usually spook the trout by noise, or by being seen. Undercut banks act as sounding boards. The trout are shy and the slightest unusual noise will send them to cover. So these fishermen conclude the trout aren't there, and they give up.

"Casting is another problem. You can do it like I did, or use a long rod and merely dap the fly into the brook and let it drift a short distance, or feed line through the guides and get a longer drift. A short drift usually is all that's necessary.

"Brooks like this always contain small trout because big ones spawn in such places. The best time is late fall when the spawners run up small brooks from rivers and lakes. I only kill males then, and only a very few because I think fishing is for fun rather than for meat.

"Another good time to fish these places," he continued, "is during mid-summer when bigger streams are too warm. Check their temperatures. When they get too warm the trout come into places like this because of the cooler water. Of course they also come into more open brooks then. Spinning tackle isn't much good here due to the casting problem. Use a long fly rod with a short, strong leader, and fish either with natural terrestrial baits or their imitations. I prefer my little bees, but grasshoppers or grubs also are good."

SOUTHERN RIVERS AND CANALS

Many areas, particularly in the South, have short rivers or drainage canals created by the United States Army Corps of Engineers. Some of these are made by dams; some are made by draining swampy areas. In parts of Florida's Everglades, many square miles of waterland have been crisscrossed by ditches and canals to provide dry land for people to build on. Since this isn't a book about ecology we won't go farther into that except to say that some of these operations have resulted in waterways of considerable angling interest.

Bonnet Areas in Drainage Canals

In southern rivers and canals we find masses of lily pads (known as "bonnets"). These often grow in bands of varying width some distance from the shoreline. The strip of water between the bonnets and the bank is often productive of all sorts of gamefish. The water on the far side of the pads is generally deeper, but it may be as deep as six to eight feet inside the pad line. Southern crappie are easiest to take in late winter and early spring. Bluegills (bream) also are found in the pads or just inside or outside of them. Schooling bass will often chase bait near the line on either side.

Angler hefts a nice crappie he took from a southern drainage canal with ample swatches of lily pads. The best water is just where he's fishing — between the pad line and the shore.

Bass water in southern Florida usually contains dense stands of sawgrass and cattails. Best fishing is along the edges of vegetation and in pockets of open water.

Grass Areas in Drainage Canals

Flood control canals connect or drain many southern lakes, some being dammed where they flow into salt or brackish water to afford fishing for snook, baby tarpon and other species on the saltwater side of the small dam and freshwater fishing for bass and pondfish on the other. The photo shows typical bass and panfish water in southern Florida. This sort of waterway usually contains dense stands of cattails, sawgrass, lily pads or other vegetation. These canals are of fairly recent origin and provide what their exponents like to call "conservation areas"—shallow impoundments built to conserve water and to prevent flooding. Typically, the canal itself may be quite deep, but the water may be shallow on the marsh side, depending on the amount of water being held by the impoundment. The other side is the dike side, and is usually a steep drop-off. In cool weather the marsh side can be especially productive because it contains considerable submerged growth in addition to what is visible on top. There are many miles of canals like this in Florida. The best fishing is along the edges of the growths and in pockets of open water.

Cyprus swamp canal is another productive type of water for bass and panfish. The best time to fish it is when the swamp has almost drained and all the baitfish are in the canal.

Cypress Swamp Canals

Another type of canal in southern regions borders a cypress swamp. Such canals support wide varieties of vegetation and thus are havens for panfish and bass. The best time to fish them is when the swamp has almost drained and baitfish have been forced to leave the swamp for the canal proper. The near side of this ditch is shallow because the dike is set well back from it. Water depths vary on the other side, providing some places where airboats or light skiffs can penetrate the swamp.

Although there are cold spells even in the South, water temperature is not as critical to fishing as it is farther north. Temperatures in Gulf Coast states average between 65 and 70 degrees, which is about in the middle of the ideal range for largemouth bass, yellow bass, white bass, drum, channel catfish, warmouth, spotted bass and crappie.

4

How Water Temperatures Affect Fishing

Experienced fishermen agree that a thermometer or temperature probe is an important piece of equipment. In Chapter 1 we noted that fish are like people in seeking comfortable temperatures. Trout and bass especially seek very specific temperatures, and cannot tolerate water of more than a few degrees variance. Members of the pike family (northern pike, muskellunge and pickerel), on the other hand, are contented in a much wider temperature range.

Science has provided us with definite information on the water temperatures preferred by various species of fish. When this was mentioned in Chapter 1, a "Temperature-Activity Table for Freshwater Fish" was given showing ideal temperatures preferred by the most important species and the surrounding range in which they can exist with reasonable comfort if they have to. This is restated in depth here for emphasis and clarification. We note that bluegills and sunfish prefer water at 74 degrees, which is usually near the surface in summer, but that they can be reasonably contented between 65 and 80 degrees. At the other end of the scale we see that lake trout prefer water of 41 degrees, but are more or less contented in a range between 40 and 50. This range is in the depths of lakes in summer, so we have to fish deep. We will find lake trout on or near the surface after the ice goes out in the spring or before freeze-up in the fall because then their preferred temperature range is on or near the surface. The trick is to fish at the ideal depth for whatever species we seek, knowing that we may not hit it exactly but that, if we are close to it, we should be reasonably successful.

What happens when fish can't find ideal temperatures, or a range in which they are reasonably comfortable? Let's take brook trout as an example. The ideal temperature for them is 58 degrees, and they should be active in streams of about that temperature, or at that temperature depth in ponds and lakes. They can get along in a range between 48 and 68 de-

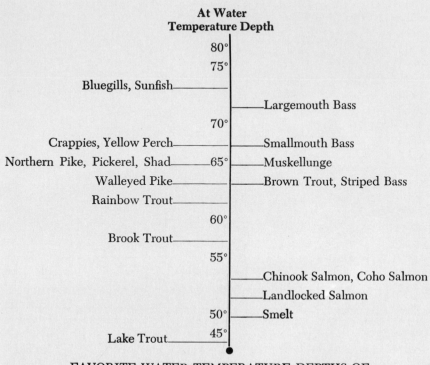

**At Water
Temperature Depth**

80°
75°
Bluegills, Sunfish————
————Largemouth Bass
70°
Crappies, Yellow Perch————
————Smallmouth Bass
Northern Pike, Pickerel, Shad————65°————Muskellunge
Walleyed Pike————
————Brown Trout, Striped Bass
Rainbow Trout————
60°
Brook Trout————
55°
————Chinook Salmon, Coho Salmon
————Landlocked Salmon
50°————Smelt
Lake Trout————45°

**FAVORITE WATER TEMPERATURE DEPTHS OF
PRINCIPAL SPECIES**

NOTE: These temperatures are close enough for good fishing, but may vary slightly between northern and southern regions due to acclimation. Tolerant temperatures vary a few degrees above and below the optimum ones given here. Members of the pike family acclimate themselves to a wide range of temperatures.

grees, but are less and less inclined to take baits and lures as water temperature deviates from the ideal. So suppose we're fishing when the trout season opens in the North and water temperature is near freezing, as it often is. Since this is below their tolerant range, and they can't find water any warmer, the trout are more or less dormant, and disinterested in baits and lures. The only way to take them then is to present small lures or baits (preferably the latter) within inches of their mouths, but their metabolism is so low that they may not take even then. Under such icy-water conditions I have seen big trout lying in the grass of high water near surface close to shore, so cold they wouldn't move away unless prodded. They were in such shallow, exposed places to seek the slight comfort of partially sun-warmed surface water there, but one could tickle their noses with a bait or lure without result.

Yet opening days on a trout stream have such fascination for anglers that they get up long before dawn to be at their favorite spots by sunup. They may give up by midmorning because ice freezes in line guides and they've had poor luck. The smart ones sleep late; arrive on streams nearer noon, and are more successful because the sun (if there is any) has warmed the water a bit.

Conversely, when water is above 68 degrees, and too warm for trout, they hug bottom where it may be cooler, or they seek cold-water brooks or spring holes. Anglers who have taken stream temperatures know this, and avoid fishing warm-water areas. Trout that can't find cool water may die, because overly warm water is deficient in oxygen.

HOW TO LOCATE CORRECT TEMPERATURE DEPTHS

Scientists have proved that fish can accurately seek their ideal temperatures to within a small fraction of a degree. This is a relatively thin stratum in deep water. Getting lures down to it becomes complicated for two reasons. Even if we know the exact depth (which instruments can tell us), trolling at that precise depth entails a consideration of boat speed, lure and line weight, length of line out, and so forth. In the next chapter we will discuss instruments that make it easier to troll at the proper depth.

Secondly, there is a certain amount of flexibility to temperature tables because fish in different parts of the country become acclimated to slightly different temperatures. For example, a largemouth bass in the South, due to heredity, may be contented in water of nearly 80 degrees while one in New England may be more used to the 72-degree temperature given here.

Water thermometers for measuring surface temperatures are inexpensive and widely available. All these tell us, however, is whether or not water near the surface approaches the ideal for the kind of fish we seek. If it does, near-surface fishing should be good in areas which satisfy other requirements of fish. If it doesn't, we'll have to work lures along the bottom in streams, fish deeper in lakes, or go somewhere else where near-surface temperatures are more suitable.

When surface temperatures are too cold in rivers or streams, lures must be fished on or near the bottom. They should be small, and worked or drifted slowly. At such times fish feed sparingly; they won't move far or at all to take lures, and usually take only small ones that require minimum exertion.

Water thermometers for measuring temperatures down deeper cost more because they are more complicated, but they are more useful. A typical one is shown here. It is about the size of a two-cell flashlight, with a dial at one end. A coil of wire, wound around it, is exposed by pulling both ends. The end of the wire is attached to a probe and a weight. By unwinding the wire the probe and weight are lowered until the desired temperature depth is reached, as recorded on the dial. This depth is marked in feet by reading the markings on the wire at water level.

Let's say, for example, that we are fishing a lake for rainbow trout. The temperature table tells us that the ideal temperature for rainbows is 61 degrees, so we lower the probe and weight until the dial reads 61 degrees. The measured wire says that this depth is 24 feet, so we know that is the

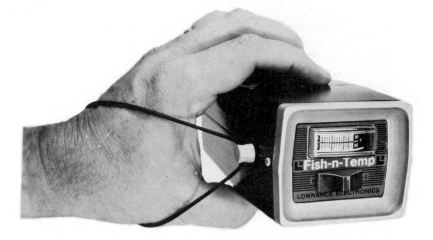

The Fish-N-Temp portable electronic thermometer is a valuable tool for determining water temperature at different depths. Depth is measured with wire probe, which records temperature on dial.

depth to be fished. In general, we fish that depth where it touches bottom, the sides of the lake, or islands or reefs. The next chapter will explain this in detail.

HOW LAKE TURNOVER AFFECTS FISHING

When taking temperature readings in lakes and deep ponds in summer, we may be surprised to find that the temperature drops sharply at a certain depth. This level of rapid temperature change is called the "thermocline," and it usually is the best place to fish then.

Water is heaviest (of greatest density) when it is at a temperature of 39.2 degrees F. Colder or warmer water is lighter and thus tends to rise to the surface and displace the heavier water, which sinks. This causes drastic changes to occur in lakes year-round. The illustrations show what happens during each season.

In winter an insulating blanket of ice covers the lake; the water below it is slightly above the freezing temperature of 32 degrees. Below this the water becomes gradually warmer (and heavier) until the temperature of maximum density of 39.2 degrees is reached near the bottom. The presence of this relatively warmer water explains why lakes don't freeze solid in winter.

Aquatic plants provide food for baitfish, which in turn provide food for larger fish. But water plants need sunlight, which helps them to absorb carbon dioxide and to gixe off oxygen in order to grow. There is a depth in deep lakes below which sufficient sunlight does not penetrate. This depth depends on the clarity of the water and the amount of snow on the ice. Since at and below this depth there is insufficient plant life and oxygen, very few fish will be found there.

These facts provide tips on where to fish through the ice. We know that, in very cold water, fish seek the warmest temperatures they can find where there is also plant life to provide food and oxygen. These two conditions are met at the greatest depth where plant life exists, so we should cut our ice-fishing holes at the two positions marked A. In shallow lakes the deepest parts would be best, but structure, discussed in the next chapter, has a bearing on this. Since proper depth varies from lake to lake, we have to locate it by trial and error. A sounding can be taken of the depth of a productive hole, and other holes bored where the lake's contour is at this depth.

Hot spots for ice fishing are found where reefs rise from the lake bottom into a level of sufficient oxygen. They are found where underground springs pour relatively warmer water into the lake, and where there are other bottom structures such as stream channels or sharp drop-offs.

As the spring sun warms the ice it gradually melts and then suddenly disappears. This is the beginning of the "spring turnover period," which is of major importance to anglers. The increasing warmth of early spring raises the water surface temperature from near freezing to 39.2 degrees. At this time all of the water in the lake is of approximately equal (and maximum) density. A wind blowing on the lake can therefore mix the surface water

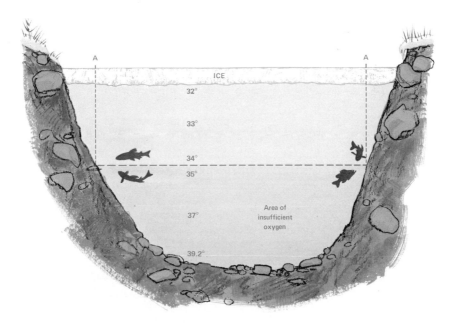

Winter stagnation. Fish are at warmest depth where there is sufficient oxygen and plant life. Ice fishermen must find this depth by trial and error, then drill other holes at same depth.

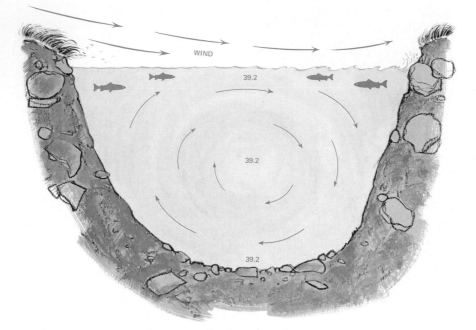

Spring turnover. The sun melts the ice and warms the water until it reaches maximum density of 39.2 degrees. Winds mix the water, equalizing the temperature; fish come to the surface to feed.

with the deeper water, actually causing all the water in the lake to churn, or to "turn over."

When this happens, equalizing the temperature of the lake, fish that have been in the depths come to the surface and feed ravenously to make up for their period of semistarvation during the winter. In New England and other northern regions, fishermen wait for the call that "the ice is out," and hurriedly pack for a quick trip to their favorite lake. They may arrive a week or more too early! The fact that the ice has left doesn't mean that the lake has turned over, bringing hungry gamefish to the top. Winds turn the lakes over, and it may take a week or more after the ice goes out for this to happen. Find out when good fishing starts, and go there then.

In the illustration the wind is blowing surface food to the eastern shore of the lake, so this shoreline should be most productive. But the surface water, barely over 39.2 degrees, is still too cold for most species of fish. So they rest and feed in shallow areas where the sun has warmed the surface water.

On many early-season trips I have found big fish lying as close as they can get to the shoreline, often in water too shallow for boats. The trick is to run the boat slowly within casting distance of the shoreline and to cast in as far as possible. Large fish may be lying in water almost too shallow to float them.

The spring turnover stage and the fall turnover stage (wherein this process is reversed) are the two times when cold-water fish such as lake trout and landlocked salmon can be caught near the surface.

As spring progresses into summer, the surface water becomes increasingly warmer. Since it is warmer, and thus lighter than the water below, it stays on top. This warm layer meets colder water below at a depth of twenty feet or more, depending on the size of the lake and weather conditions. Where the warm layer meets the cold layer, a certain amount of mixing occurs, forming a third, intermediate layer. This middle layer may be twenty feet or more thick, again depending on lake size and weather conditions. In any pond or lake, the temperature of this intermediate layer remains constant all summer long. It is called the "thermocline," and it is the level of good fishing.

In choosing where they will spend the summer, cold-water fish shun the lower layer because it contains insufficient oxygen and food. They shun the upper layer because it is too warm. Thus they cruise in or very near the thermocline level where the temperature preference of each individual species suits it best.

In staying at this level they also want to be near protection and food, which means that they usually will be found where this level meets the sides of the lake, or at this depth around islands and submerged reefs. They may leave this level to come nearer the surface where cold-water streams

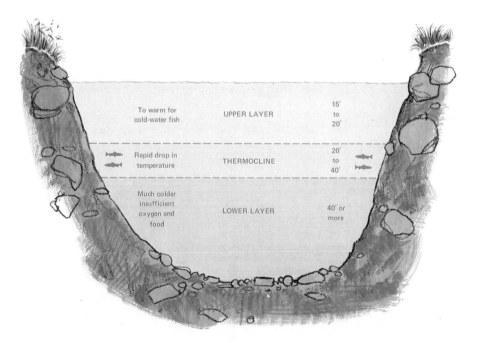

To warm for cold-water fish	UPPER LAYER	15' to 20'
Rapid drop in temperature	THERMOCLINE	20' to 40'
Much colder insufficient oxygen and food	LOWER LAYER	40' or more

Summer stratification. Lake stratifies into three layers. Top layer is too warm, bottom layer lacks sufficient oxygen; fish inhabit the thermocline where temperature is constant all summer long.

enter the lake and, under certain conditions, they may come into the shallows of warmer water in the evening or during the night to feed. However, in summer, the thermocline level usually is our best bet.

We have seen that we can find the thermocline level by taking readings at increasing depths with a temperature probe. For the first twenty feet or so readings at five-foot intervals will be very much the same. Then suddenly the instrument will indicate a rapid drop in temperature. The water will become rapidly colder as increasingly deeper readings are taken, and then the readings will level off when the probe goes below the thermocline level. (The thermocline, technically, is the layer where the drop in temperature is at least one degree Centigrade per meter of depth.)

Thus, for the best summer fishing, we should stillfish or troll at the thermocline level where this level is near the edge of the lake bottom. If we can obtain a contour map of the lake (or want to bother to make one) we can chart the path of good trolling which, in a simple example, might look something like the accompanying diagram. We know the preferred water temperature of the fish we want to catch; now we are all set to translate this knowledge into action.

Shallow lakes or ponds may not stratify; long, narrow ones may stratify in the deep parts but not in the shallow. If no stratification is found, the answer is to fish the deeper parts because they are cooler, and springs there may make certain areas comfortable for fish. Inlet streams provide cooler water, so their mouths may be hot spots in summer.

HOW TO FISH SMALL LAKES IN SUMMER

Study the accompanying map, provided by the Massachusetts Fish and Game Department, of a typical pond. Our temperature probe says the thermocline area is between twenty and twenty-five feet deep. By coloring in the areas between these two contours, the "path of good trolling" can be established. This is where the twenty- to twenty-five-foot depth touches the sides of the lake, its islands and reefs. By noting shoreline characteristics and reading the map, we can follow this path in a boat with reasonable accuracy. Simple maps such as this, or more elaborate ones, with contour lines marked for depths, are obtainable from state fish and game departments, the U. S. Geological Survey, and other sources, and usually can be purchased in sporting goods stores. It is advisable to fish one lake and learn its hot spots and other secrets, for fish concentrations and habits will vary from place to place.

This map reveals more than the paths of good trolling. It indicates steep drop-offs, which often are hot spots. These can be fished deep with bait, jigs or plastic worms. The map points out shoal areas which may harbor aquatic plants; these are excellent areas for panfish and bass which feed in the shallows at dusk. Suitable water temperatures may induce gamefish to remain in the shallows for longer periods.

Such a shallow area is shown in the photo on page 84. Gamefish may lie in the protection of the weeds but most often will be found in the open pockets and along the weed lines. Weedless lures can be drawn slowly

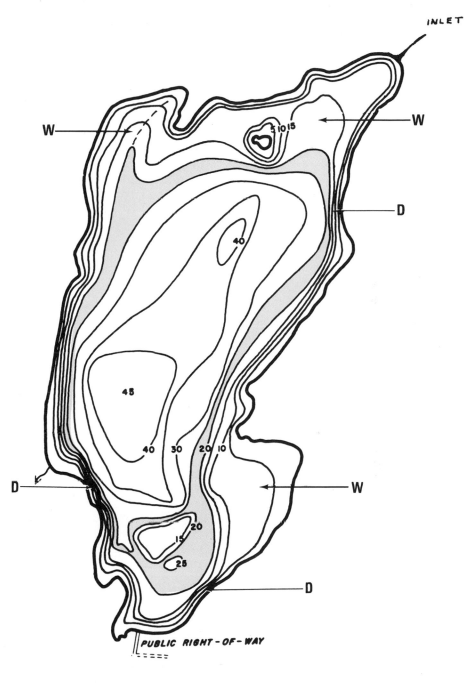

This map of a pond has been shaded to show the path of good trolling in the thermocline. Steep drop-offs, hot spots for jigging, are at points marked *D*. Deep hole at twenty-five feet should be fished, also the inlet if there is a moderate current. Weedy shallows where bass and panfish feed in morning and evening in warm weather are marked *W*.

Shallows of lakes which are rich in aquatic vegetation are prime feeding areas for bass and pickerel. Fish lie in openings or near the weed lines.

through the vegetation into open pockets. Big bass often notice this overhead disturbance in the weeds and pounce on the lure.

Note the deep hole near the bottom of the map where depth is about twenty-five feet. When surface water is too warm this hole may be a hot spot because it is just under the thermocline level. Probably bass lie in this hole in warm weather and migrate to the shallows northeast of it for evening feeding sprees. If there was a channel between the hole and the shallows, this would be a migratory route that should be fished carefully. We also can experiment with places a bit deeper, but ideal ones should be close to the bottom of the thermocline level.

This map provides basic information on where and how to find fish in small bodies of water and it serves as an introduction to the subject of "structure fishing," which will be discussed in following chapters. It indicates several possible migratory routes for fish, the most obvious being in the northwest corner where the twenty- to twenty-five-foot depth comes to a point as it enters the cove. If the cove is rich in food-bearing protective vegetation, fish entering it from the depths would follow the point up the base of the submerged valley into the shallows. The dashed line identifies this route on the map.

When shallower water offers suitable temperatures in spring and fall we should find gamefish around the small island in the northern part of the map. Let's assume a breeze is blowing from the west and ruffling the surface. Then, fishing around the island should be best in the lee of the eastern side. If the island is big enough to provide a large sheltered spot there, the wind will form edges on the surface where the calm and disturbed areas meet. Pay special attention to these edges because the wind may be blowing surface foods along them.

Under similar conditions the submerged island in the southern part of the map may be productive. The map shows this to be between about twelve and twenty feet deep. In summer the path of good trolling will be around the island, but in cooler weather gamefish may be feeding above it.

Without a map, all we would see of this pond would be a small island at the northern end, steep banks here and there, and a few shallows. With it, the whole structure of the pond's bottom is revealed. The path of good trolling is marked. We see numerous potential hot spots that distinguish good areas from poor ones, helping us to find fish and to make excursions on the pond productive.

FINDING CORRECT TROLLING DEPTH

Later we will discuss trolling with sophisticated equipment that tows baits or lures at the desired depth. Here, let's see what can be done with almost nothing—a plumb line of a hundred feet or so marked at five-foot intervals, with enough weight on its end to drop it straight to the bottom.

Since various combinations of lines, lures, leads, etc. will troll at varying depths, let's learn the capabilities of only one set to start with. Spinning tackle will twist monofilament badly unless the necessary steps are taken to prevent it. Rigs made for trolling do nicely, but my favorite is more unusual. It is a low-cost fiberglass fly rod about 8½ feet long with a large and sturdy fly reel containing two or three hundred feet of fine monel wire line. The forward part of the line is marked every 25 feet. Swiveled to the end of the wire is at least fifty feet of twenty-pound-test monofilament, to which is tied about ten feet of ten-pound-monofilament, with the lure attached to the end.

I know about how much wire line to let out for the desired fishing depth, and there is a speed indicator on the power boat to insure trolling at the correct and steady speed which, of course, is influenced by the force and direction of the wind. If there are no strikes with the amount of line out, some can be taken in or let out until strikes occur. I troll with a measured speed, until there is reason to change. The amount is estimated from jottings in a notebook containing previous data.

The advantage of this method is that, when a fish is hooked, the wire line can be reeled in and the fish can be played on the monofilament, as one would do in fly fishing. If the lure becomes caught on the bottom and can't be freed, the light ten-pound tippet breaks, thus saving the rest of the tackle.

One can't guess trolling speed accurately but inexpensive devices such as the Trolex are available for measuring speed. Correct speed is about five miles per hour, or about as fast as a man can walk.

So far, then, to troll at correct depth, we should get used to one set of tackle with the same lures and we should troll at constant speed. All that remains is to know how much line to put out.

Since lures should usually be trolled close to bottom, a maxim is that one isn't trolling deep enough unless the lure snags occasionally. When this happens, get directly above the snagged lure and measure its depth with the plumb line previously mentioned. For example, we want to troll at thirty feet and have a hundred and fifty feet of wire line out, but, when we get hung up and use the plumb line, we find the depth to be only twenty feet. A rough formula here is that five feet of line adds one foot of depth, but this varies according to line weight, trolling speed, etc., so we have to work out the formula that suits our tackle. A few hang-ups can establish this and, if we record the data, we'll learn the formula. In this case let's let fifty more feet of line out, which should be about correct.

If the path of good trolling is at thirty feet, we can let out a hundred and fifty feet of line, but this should be extended gradually until we feel the lure bouncing bottom. At this point, reel in a little to keep the lure from bouncing constantly, but let out or take in line once in a while to probe the bottom by letting the lure touch it. Use lures or baits of about the same weight and drag (water resistance). Lighter and/or more streamlined lures will tend to troll higher, and vice versa.

When fall arrives and cold nights lower surface water temperatures, the reverse of the spring turnover stage takes place. When surface water has cooled to 39.2 degrees all the water in the pond or lake is of such similar density that wind action can mix it and equalize it at 39.2 degrees. Since the thermocline and the warm upper layer then no longer exist, the fish which have been living at thermocline level, or near it, now come to the surface again and can be caught on top. Cold-water fish, such as lake trout, coho and landlocked salmon, provide top sport with surface lures around islands, reefs and shorelines. The fall turnover stage lasts until ice begins to form.

When the ice begins to form the winter stagnation period sets in and the annual cyclic behavior of northern lakes is completed.

Thus, if we want to fish for cold-water species, the best times to do it for greatest sport are during the weeks in the spring and in the fall when no thermal stratification exists and they can be caught on or near the surface. At such times they are more lively than during summer or winter and provide better sport.

5

Structure: Another Secret of Finding Fish

Knowing and locating the temperatures fish seek reduces our search for productive water in lakes to a small fraction of the whole. Now, let's reduce it further, eliminating perhaps ninety-five percent. The other five percent is where most of the fish are.

This elimination of unproductive water has to do with the structure of lakes. "Structure fishing" is the system of studying the underwater habitats of fish to determine where to find most of them. Expert anglers have always understood structure fishing to some extent, but the fairly recent development of electronic depth-locating devices and temperature probes has taken a lot of guesswork out of the game. It has been said that we can find structure without fish, but we can't find fish without structure.

Underwater structures that harbor fish are of two kinds—natural and man-made. The latter are usually found in artificial lakes and reservoirs. Some structures are visible on or from the surface, or can be deduced by land characteristics, such as a creek channel, a deep ditch or a small valley going into a lake, or a point of land. Other structures, being much deeper, can only be located by electronic depth-measuring devices such as the Fish Lo-K-Tor.

NATURAL STRUCTURES

Stream Beds
Channels of streams often extend far out into lakes, usually dispersing into their depths. When lakes have been raised by dams or have been created as impoundments these channels are usually long and distinct. Impoundments are often made by dams raised over river beds. In this case the main channel usually extends the entire length of the impoundment, and into it, vein-like, come the smaller channels of what formerly were tributary streams and brooks. All of these are structures which may harbor fish, but parts of them are much better than others.

Lowrance Electronics, Inc.

This submerged stream bed in an impoundment is marked by dead trees whose trunks appear above the surface. Note the sharp bend in the channel where the outside curve drops off deeply. This structure, which can be pinpointed with a Fish Lo-K-Tor, is usually a hot spot for gamefish.

One place is where the former stream bed (now deeply hidden in the lake) makes a sharp bend, forming a deep hole on the outside. These holes are important fish-holding structures. Another is the junction where a smaller stream joins a bigger one. The deep holes usually found at such junctions can also be important fish-holding structures.

Maps made of the area before it became an impoundment show the streams and their characteristics. If such a map is contoured, the shape of the impoundment can be drawn in. Actual locations can be estimated by sightings of landmarks above the surface. Depth probes such as a sinker on a measured line can pinpoint them more exactly.

A better way is to locate such places with an electronic depth probe such as the Lo-K-Tor. The best way is to use a contour map with the depth probe.

Such channels often act as migratory routes between holding areas in deep water and feeding areas in the shallows, but more about that later. We know that water temperatures have a distinct influence on fish and how they use these routes, and that temperatures vary from season to season.

Deep Holes and Migratory Routes
Contour maps of lakes often show holes of varying size and depth caused by topographical adjustments not associated with channels. When these holes have hard bottoms, and when the water there contains sufficient oxygen and is of suitable temperature, they can be valuable holding areas for fish. Well-equipped anglers can locate these holes with instruments mentioned in this book, but the only way to determine whether they hold fish is to explore them with jigs or bottom-bumping lures. If a hole doesn't produce, mark it down for trial under more favorable circumstances, and move on to another structure.

When water in deep holes is of proper temperature and contains sufficient oxygen, the holes can be suitable bedrooms for fish, but they may be inadequate as dining rooms. Fish rest comfortably there, but they have to migrate to less comfortable and perhaps more exposed places to feed. Thus they establish migratory routes between resting and feeding spots which, in the case of largemouth bass, for example, may be in grassy, weedy or lily-pad areas in shallows close to shore. Other fish, such as trout, may prefer to feed on reefs or bars. Anyway, the migratory route usually is the easiest way to travel from place to place—a stream bed, a gully or a gradual slope rather than a steep one. Contour maps may indicate probable migratory routes. Fish going into shallows to feed usually take these routes in late afternoon, returning when they have fed, or as late as early the next morning. Many anglers like to fish these routes at proper times, and they often are very successful.

Points of Land
Favorite spots of mine are easy-to-locate points of land which shelve off deeply. Depth can be estimated by the steepness of the point. Many kinds of gamefish common to the lake, especially trout and bass, are found in such places when water temperature is suitable, because water around

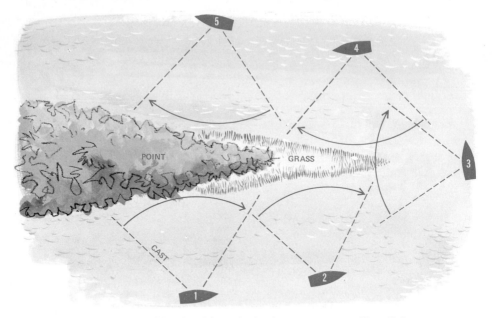

Fishing a point of land. Although the hot spot is usually off the tip, it pays to cover all the water by fan-casting from position 1 and working around to position 5. Anchor the boat at each position and cover the water thoroughly, especially grassy areas.

points also provides the other requirements of fish—a food supply if the point is grassy or bushy, the protection of vegetation and dark or shaded water, and abundant oxygen. Hot spots usually are off the tips of points. The shady side should be the better one, but it usually pays to explore the whole point thoroughly.

This is usually done by fan-casting from enough anchored positions to cover the entire point, both on or near surface and deep, as indicated in the sketch. It can be done from a slowly moving boat if one is in a hurry, but this may not allow enough time to fish the bottom properly. Keep the boat at a distance that allows you to cast lures safely into the grasses or bushes. If a hang-up occurs and you can't pull loose, consider breaking off the lure rather than going in to get it—and spoiling the water. It can probably be retrieved after the area has been fished.

Noises alarm fish, and a hot spot may seem barren after someone has tossed out the anchor or banged a tacklebox. Consider the advantage of an electric motor. Lower the anchor carefully. And try putting a springy rug on the boat's deck to deaden sounds made by feet and equipment.

Water temperature tells us whether to fish near surface or down deep. In early morning and late evening the surface may be productive anyway. If not, depth is the answer. My first choice then might be to cast a plastic worm to shore and to walk or hop it very slowly down the incline until it is under the boat. Spinner-baits, jigs, spoons and bottom-scratching plugs also pay off from time to time. Everyone has his favorite types of lures in his choices of sizes and colors, but opinions advanced by experts will be discussed later in this book.

When deeply shelving bottom structures are nearby and when points of land contain considerable surface and subsurface vegetation (with its accompanying food supply), places like this can be especially productive.

Drop-Offs to Deep Water

The closeness of surface and subsurface contour lines on topographical maps indicates steep drop-offs, which also can be found by observing where a cliff shelves steeply into the water. Topographical maps showing subsurface contours often reveal unseen drop-offs which may be even better.

Drop-offs extending down steeply from the surface are especially good when wind or breeze blows toward them. When surface water is colder than fish prefer, but when the day is warm, the surface water will heat up and the wind will blow this warmer top water toward the drop-off—in effect, piling it up there. The surface water there can be several degrees warmer than the rest of the lake, making it a sought-after place for fish.

Winds also blow surface foods toward the drop-off. These foods may be spent insects and other small things, but they attract baitfish, and thus gamefish. For these reasons drop-offs can be very productive in the colder weather of early or late season.

The drop-off shown on page 92 is typical of many hot spots in lakes. At the shoreline the point drops off into six to eight feet of water and then gently slopes toward the deeper part of the lake and the channel of the incoming stream at the left. This rock and gravel slope is ideal habitat for many species of fish but particularly for smallmouth bass and trout.

We could fish this point from a boat anchored or drifting as far out as possible, casting in to the rocks, and then working the lure down the incline. We also could cast from shore, give the lure plenty of time to sink on a loose line, and then work it in close to the bottom up the incline. If smallmouth bass are presumed to be here, a three-inch weighted plastic worm might do well if hopped up or down the incline very slowly. Spinners or wobblers should be productive for trout. When water temperatures tempt fish to the top, streamers or bucktails should do well, in sizes and colors imitating prevalent baitfish.

Coves and Thorofares

The photo on page 93 shows a thorofare which is an almost currentless, river-like passage from one lake to another. Formerly, the outlet of a higher lake entered a lower one here, but the damming of the lower lake to make a reservoir has brought both lakes to the same level. Cover the lower drawing in the picture and try to imagine its structure by looking at the photograph. The original stream bed has been greatly deepened by the flooding to provide an interesting fish-holding structure.

As this is a migratory route from one lake to the other, both baitfish and gamefish collect here. In late spring and early fall fish will travel the thoroughfare in search of better water temperatures or better spawning

Lowrance Electronics, Inc.

This gradually sloping point drops off into a channel extending into the cove at left. This is a hot spot for feeding fish. The channel is a migratory route into the cove, another good feeding area.

Lowrance Electronics, Inc.

The damming of the lake in the foreground has raised the water level and transformed the stream into a currentless thorofare between one lake and another, a migratory route for fish which should offer good fishing all season.

locations, often tarrying at this junction before passing through. The steep banks may be weedy and abundant with food. Fish probably lie in the shade of the bridge and the protection of its pilings.

An angler fishing off the bridge or near its abutments might not realize how deep the water is. He probably would try lures near the surface and then fish them a bit deeper, not realizing that his quarry would be holding or feeding close to the bottom. The trick here is to cast far out and to feel bottom while working in the lure. To get the lure down, after making the cast do not put the line back under control of the reel. Let line peel off freely so the lure will sink directly to the bottom instead of reeling it in on a tight line. Each cast should explore the bottom in this manner. When line stops peeling off, put it under control of the reel and fish it in along the bottom.

Now, let's assume that this bridge crosses a narrow arm of the lake which goes into a weedy cove. The width of the cove makes no difference; all coves are worth investigating, particularly when winds make the lake too rough for fishing.

If the cove is rich in weeds, grasses and pads, and therefore abundant in food, gamefish from the lake will often come in to feed there. When water temperatures are to their liking in the cove, or perhaps when surface waters there grow cooler in evening or early morning, the normal piscatorial population of the cove will be augmented by visitors from the lake, many of which may be of trophy size. The cove may be a hot spot for pike, or for largemouth or smallmouth bass—or for many other species when conditions are right. Catfish and their kin may be there all the time, as well as pickerel and other pondfish.

Fishing in lakes may get tiresome or impractical for one reason or another. Regardless of that, don't neglect to explore the hidden mysteries of promising coves.

Submerged Islands, Reefs and Bars

Regardless of their depth, structures protruding from a lake's bottom— submerged islands, reefs and bars—almost always produce fish. Some structures may be observed by peering into a lake through polarized glasses. Others may be discerned by a rock or two breaking the surface, or by vegetation, such as the little tree in this picture. If a point of land extends toward an island, a bar probably runs part way between.

However, most submerged structures can't be located on the surface. They can be located accurately by electronic depth-probing devices, which tell us how deep the summit of the structure is, how far it protrudes above the bottom, whether the structure is muddy or hard, and how thick is the vegetation. With a contour map and an electronic depth-probing instrument, one can quickly learn all about the bottom structures of a lake.

We now know how to find the correct temperature depth for the species of fish we seek. The idea is to fish close to bottom structures at the right depth, for fish will be lying or cruising close to them for protection and food. Contours can be marked to identify correct paths for trolling. Temperature probes tell us where to anchor and how deep to fish to hit bottom at proper levels.

Lowrance Electronics, Inc.

This submerged island is marked by a lone tree that emerges from the summit. Stumps on the bottom identify the lake as an impoundment. Often too deep to be seen from the surface, submerged islands, reefs and bars, which are hot spots, can be located with electronic depth-probing devices such as the Lowrance Fish Lo-K-Tor.

Surface markers are valuable for this, and they can be made or purchased. One type is shaped like a dumbbell and made of a brightly colored, floatable material with line wound around its waist and a weight at the end of the line. When our probing tells us we are over the right spot to hit bottom at the right depth, we drop one of these markers there. The weight quickly unwinds the line and hits bottom. Then the line is half-hitched around the marker. In fishing a reef, several of these may be dropped to mark its length. Then we can drift or troll over the area and always know we are on the right path.

When the tops of these structures (sometimes called "mounds") are at suitable temperature depth, fish may roam and feed over them, particularly when they are covered with aquatic growth. Weedy tops of relatively shallow structures are hot spots for yellow perch. Smallmouth bass hold on tops or sides of rocky or gravel structures at suitable temperature depth. Largemouth bass prefer hard bottoms.

Weedy and Grassy Areas
Pond and lake shallows which are thick with lily pads, hyacinths, grasses and weeds offer protection and food for fish. This picture of a dollar pad area in a shallow lake is a good example.

This sort of place is an ideal habitat for largemouth bass, pickerel and other pondfish; also for trout when water temperatures are agreeable to them. Largemouth bass spawn in such places in the spring, sweeping out circular depressions between the growths to expose gravel on which they lay their eggs. When the shallow water becomes too warm in summer the bass and trout leave these areas for deeper water, but they may return daily at dusk to feed and remain perhaps until sunup the next day.

Dollar pad area in a lake offers fish food and protection. Best place to fish such an area is along the weed line.

Since the weedy area shown in the picture has few open spots we have the choices of casting weedless lures at random and working them over the pads or of fishing the weed line (as marked), which probably will be more productive and more fun. Here's a tip on fishing weed lines like this:

Wade if possible, but use a silent boat if not. Cast as closely as possible to the weed line and fish the lure in along the edge. Make the first cast short, gradually extending the length of subsequent casts. This procedure hooks the nearest fish without alarming those farther away.

More fish usually lie along the weed line than amidst the growth inside of it, but if the inside has open holes, or if there are open-water cuts entering the growth from the weed line, these can be hot spots and should be fished carefully. The firm edge of weeds here indicates that there may be a drop-off along it. This would make fishing there even better.

Anglers from all over North America travel to Florida to fish for big bass in the Everglades. The sport is a way of life for fishermen near the Everglades National Park. Whether or not we've been there, or may or may not ever want to go, this unusual sort of largemouth bass fishing is packed with thrills and challenges.

The "sea of grass" which is the Everglades can be explored in part by following boat trails, but airboats are needed to reach remote areas. Don't venture far from civilization without an expert guide because it's easy to get lost.

Anglers sometimes leave their airboat and wade from open pocket to open pocket, carefully covering each one with spinning or plugcasting lures in search of big bass. Light johnboats are used wherever there are canals or boat trails. "Reading the water" usually means "reading the grass," finding potholes and other fairly open places where one can cast without getting snagged too often. When fishing narrow canals and boat trails, anglers usually cast straight ahead, covering both sides as near the grass as possible. Bass lie in the edges of the grass ready to pounce on moving bait.

Another interesting kind of southern fishing is casting for bass in flooded cypress forests or swamps. Gamefish forage in the inundated areas, which would contain no water in dry weather. When swamps are draining, the gamefish and baitfish are forced to leave, so these are the times to fish the outlet drainage canals.

MAN-MADE STRUCTURES

Impoundments created for flood control and for reservoirs are often many miles long with arms and bays which once were lowlands and valleys. In flooding the area, it may have been necessary to cover towns, villages and farms, as well as wooded lands. The result is a complex of man-made structures which become havens for fish and hot spots for fishermen. In shallow areas some of these structures can be seen from the surface. Most of them, however, are deep and must be located by maps or instruments.

Old maps of the area, made before the impoundment was created, can be used by marking the contour of the water level. This reveals the present shape of the impoundment and all that is submerged in it. Geological Sur-

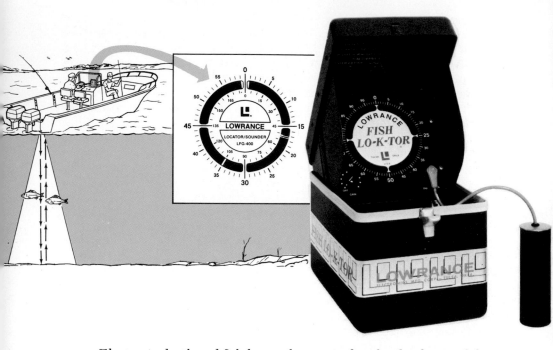

Electronic depth and fish locator has a wired probe that locates fish and bottom structure and records them on a dial. In the drawing of the dial large fish are shown to be at about seventeen feet and solid bottom at thirty-five feet.

vey maps may or may not show these details, but anglers can make such maps if regional sources don't provide them.

An electronic depth locator isn't essential but is amazingly helpful. A reliable and popular model is the Lowrance Fish Lo-K-Tor. This battery-operated device (rechargeable at home) transmits and receives sonar sound waves. These waves are projected into the water in a cone-shaped pattern. When they hit an object within the pattern they are reflected back so the depth can be read on the dial. The instrument can tell when the boat is over or approaching individual fish or schools of fish, as well as their depth and the depth of the water under the boat.

Units of this sort are usually effective to a depth of 120 feet, and under favorable conditions (sand, gravel or rock bottoms) can be read at twice that depth. They are effective in salt or muddy water, as well as for fishing through the ice. Fishermen who know how to use them to locate individual fish or schools of fish, record their depth and the depth of the bottom, can also learn to estimate the *size* of the fish and determine the *character* of the bottom. While such an instrument is expensive, there is little or no cost of maintenance, and it is a very valuable aid to the chronic lake fisherman. Let's look at one of many jobs a depth locator can perform.

A Submerged Bridge Crossing a Channel

Our contour map shows a former road that crosses a former stream bed by a now deeply submerged bridge, the deck of which was left when the impoundment was flooded. We see from shore where the road enters the lake, and the map gives the approximate distance to the bridge. Experience tells us that the channel made by the former stream, where it passes under the bridge, should be a sanctuary for big bass, which also may use the stream bed and the road bed as migratory routes.

Dead reckoning takes us as near this presumed hot spot as visual sightings and estimation can, but this isn't close enough because we must be exactly over the sides of the bridge. We turn on the depth locator. The flashes on the dial indicating lake bottom suddenly show the bottom to be twenty feet deeper than usual. By running the boat in S-curves we know by the markings flashing on the dial that we are over the old channel, and we pinpoint its direction. While we're cruising over the channel the locator suddenly shows blips indicating something solid below. We think we are over the bridge, and absence of blips over those indicating the bottom suddenly confirm that we have passed over it. We return and probably drop a marker onto the bridge itself so we can return to the exact spot.

We now know the exact location of the bridge, the depth of its deck and the channel beneath. We can anchor or drift just up-channel or down-channel from the floating marker and jig or bounce our lures beside the bridge deck into the channel below it. We can cast plastic worms or other lures to the drainage ditch beside the road and walk or hop them down the incline to the bottom of the old stream bed. If this really is a hot spot, we should have strikes right away, and the chances are that we will load our stringer in short order.

Submerged Roadbeds

While fishing this spot, let's look around a little. The map snows the direction of the submerged road, and we can see that it goes through a deep cut before making a curve indicated on the map. This sort of deep structure is ideal for bass, so the plan now is to troll over the old roadbed and to bounce lures close to the road itself. After we pass through the cut our Lo-K-Tor will keep us on course. Quick, sharp blips on the dial show that we are passing over fish—a signal to be ready when the trolled lures reach them. If there are no strikes, let's make another pass over the roadbed, using different lures.

Causeways

A causeway is a raised road—for example, a road built on fill along a river or over swampland. Causeways are often productive structures for bass and other gamefish.

Our map shows that a typical causeway runs along the river. In this instance it probably can be traced by the elevation of ground above lake level, part of which was bulldozed to make the road. Anyway, our Lo-K-Tor shows it, and where it falls away to the former stream bed. The road and the stream bed both are excellent structures for trolling or casting, but we

Lowrance Electronics, Inc.

Submerged bridge across a former stream bed, as well as the road-way and drainage ditch, are the type of fishy bottom structures shown on a contour map. An electronic depth locator is needed to pinpoint them.

know that the most productive parts of the stream bed are the deeper outside curves.

The road may run across a depression which had to be filled in to make a complete causeway, and this may contain a bridge or two, which should be indicated on the map. The low area on each side of the causeway could provide excellent fishing.

One might say that this is a rather extensive area to fish. Some parts of the area should be better than others, but even the poorest parts offer better structure than most of the impoundment. Many anglers say that only about five percent of a natural lake or an impoundment is worth fishing. We are trying to identify the various types of structures that make up that important five percent, so the rest can be ignored.

Rock-Fill

Rock-fill is used to support causeways, as rip-rapping along the bank of a stream, or to strengthen land-fill. Such rocky places are havens for baitfish, since they provide shade, protection and food. The rock-fill in the accompanying photo is a known crayfish habitat. At sundown, crayfish crawl from their hideouts in the underwater rocks to forage the lake bottom for food. Gamefish should be nearby. Lures imitating crayfish (or baitfish) should bring strikes here, and casts should be made as close as possible to the rocks, which may harbor large fish in their crevices.

Rock-fill jutting into a deep part of this lake is a haven for crayfish — and gamefish should be nearby.

Dams

Fishing may not be allowed near dams in reservoirs, but if so, the dam may be a hot spot. While we are exploring dammed impoundments, it often pays to drop a temperature probe near the dam. Jigging or baitfishing at the right temperature depth should produce results. If we have a Fish Lo-K-Tor on the boat it may pay to drift around a bit while watching the dial. The dial will indicate depths showing whether the bottom shelves off sharply or is more rounded. It will also show the presence and depth of large and small fish.

Standing Timber and Brush

In certain parts of the country anglers refer to underwater mazes of brush and timber as "stump ranches" or "stick-ups." They are usually found in man-made lakes that have been created by damming creek channels. If the lake contains bass they will seek cover in places like this during the cool weather of spring and fall, particularly if the water is shallow. In summer they may come here from deeper water to feed in the evening and at night, returning to the depths at sunup. If the water is deeper, bass may be here at all times. Rainbow and brown trout often gravitate to this type

Sawed-off stumps in an impoundment provide good cover for bass and trout. This is perfect water for fishing popping bugs for bass.

of cover because it contains an abundance of minnows and large aquatic insects. In the South such places may abound with crappies.

This is ideal water for using fly-rod popper bugs for panfish and large-mouth bass. It also is excellent for live bait such as hellgrammites fished just off bottom on a small bobber. When streamer flies or nymphs are fished deep, the barbs should be protected with looped monofilament weed guards or they should be tied on Keel hooks. Casts should be directed to open spots close to the stumps.

A similar structural situation is offered by brush piles, which are prevalent in many southern lakes. In fishing Lake Ouachita, in Arkansas, we found that crappies, bass and other pondfish were most prevalent in two places—off grassy points of land and near brush piles. The brush was rooted to bottom ten feet deep. The best lure proved to be a weighted six-inch weedless red plastic worm. The trick was to cast a short distance into any fairly open place in the brush, to let the worm sink to bottom, and to crawl it slowly back to the boat. We lost a good many lures, but we returned to the dock with limits of fish!

HOW TO FISH AN IMPOUNDMENT

While impoundments in unsettled areas have natural structures, which have been discussed, they of course lack man-made structures such as roads, bridges, house foundations, etc. Let's look at a major impoundment in a formerly settled area and see how to find the hot spots.

The map on pages 104-105 shows part of Quabbin Reservoir in central Massachusetts, an impoundment of 38 square miles of water, 18 miles long, 7 miles wide (at the widest point), with a maximum depth of 150 feet. The top of its summer thermocline is about 30 feet below the surface and it is about 20 feet thick. Since the water is clear, fish may be well below thermocline depth at favorite water temperature levels.

All the structure in Quabbin was carefully mapped before flooding early in this century, the map sections being scaled at 200 feet to an inch. Anglers who fish there successfully specialize in one small section or another to learn its hidden possibilities. These successful anglers often return with limit catches of big fish while casual ones, who don't understand the structure they are fishing over, usually do poorly. Introduced smelt provide the major food supply. Introduced or indigenous gamefish are brook, brown, rainbow and lake trout, landlocked salmon, largemouth, smallmouth and white bass, walleyed pike and panfish. The trout occupy areas unsuited for bass, which we know prefer depths near shallow feeding areas. The small section of the reservoir shown in the map on pages 104-105 shows how the structure looks when magnified to the scale of 200 feet to an inch.

The combination of water temperature and structure is the secret of finding fish here as well as in other places. In summer (August) water surface temperature is about 72 degrees. This drops slightly to 70 degrees at the top of the thermocline at 30 feet below surface level. From 30 to 50 feet of depth the temperature drop is one degree per foot or to 50 degrees at 50 feet of depth. Below the thermocline's bottom at 50 feet the tempera-

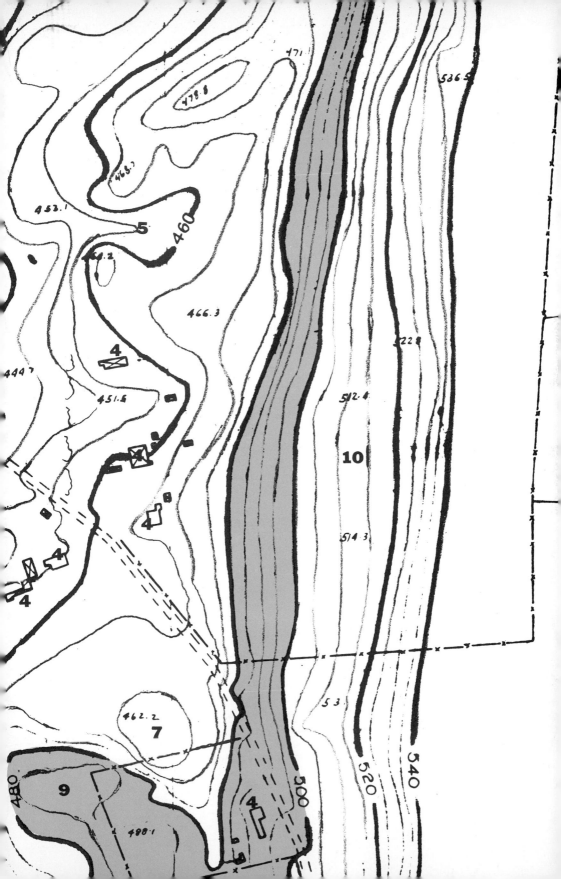

ture decrease to the lake's floor at greatest depth of about 150 feet is very slight (only 2 or 3 degrees), perhaps because the lake's bottom water is drawn off for water supply purposes. In interpreting the map we also should note that at this time the lake is 530 feet above sea level, so all depths marked on the map should be increased by 10 feet. Thus, in fishing for brown, brook and rainbow trout, whose favorite water temperatures are between 58 and 63 degrees, we are interested in the 50 to 70 degree thermocline level whose contours are marked between 480 and 500 feet, or between 30 and 50 feet of depth. Landlocked salmon fishing should be best just below the thermocline, and lake trout can be at maximum depths because this lake is clear and well oxygenated. For reasons stated, this is not a good bass area.

With the hope that readers understand this briefing, let's look at some of the more obvious structures. Here, these are at temperature depths most interesting to lake trout fishermen, but the same types of structures are generally noteworthy because they would harbor other species in shallower lakes with warmer water.

The most interesting structure here is the old river channel, and particularly its numerous sharp bends (1) in the valley which now is a depression in the lake's bottom. In a shallower and warmer lake these sharp bends would be excellent substructures for bass and other fish. Here, they should be lairs for lake trout and landlocked salmon. Another hot spot in the channel is the bridge (2) crossing the river bed.

Between contour lines 440 and 420 are several steep dropoffs (3), a bit too cold except for lake trout and salmon here, but interesting structures in warmer lakes. The same is true of several cellar holes (4); ideal for bass under warmer conditions. Narrow valleys (5) and a road structure up a valley (6) also are of interest, as well as a large depression (7), which may be the bed of a former pond. A valley and its minor stream bed can be seen at (8) and a large mound (9) is at the right temperature level to be a good holding area for brook, brown and rainbow trout. In many lakes all these would be valuable fish-holding structures.

If this particular map should be used to locate brook, brown or rainbow trout, the best area would be between contour lines 480 and 500, where the drop-off of the shoreline is between 30 and 50 feet deep and the water temperature varies between 50 and 70 degrees. In this case this is the thermocline area and its temperature is correct for trout. The area has been shaded on the map to indicate the path of good trolling, but lures fished up or down the drop-off could be productive. Important structures in this thermocline area are the former road and the cellar hole near the bottom of the map. The road would be a migratory route (particularly for bass) if it led to feeding shallows. I don't know that the drop-off between contours 480 and 500 actually is a hot spot for trout but an almost identical drop-off on the other side of this arm of the lake is a famous place for catching the big ones. If surface waters are cooler in summer or relatively warm in spring and fall, trout may venture farther up the drop-off (10) to the surface and particularly into shallow areas offering protection.

The 50-degree temperature level (near the bottom of the thermocline, here) is a favorite one for migrations of American smelt, the principal food in this and many other lakes. Smelt follow shorelines at this level, which is a reason why gamefish should be there also.

This portion of the map of the vast Quabbin Reservoir was selected because it shows a variety of the actual structures which this book has discussed, structures which can be hot spots for all kinds of fishing when water temperatures are suitable. On this map stone walls, former tree lines, fences and swamps are also indicated. Impoundments are usually mapped before they are flooded, and the maps should be available from their headquarters.

HOW TO TROLL DEEP AT CORRECT DEPTH

Most readers will do well enough trolling by following the suggestions that have been offered. Those who fish from a power boat on a large, deep lake may be interested in a new product, the Lowrance LTG-200 Fish-N-Temp Rig. It consists of a reel of 200 feet of 95-pound-test cable at the end of which is a 7½-pound hydrodynamic weight. A quick-release device frees the fishing line attached to the weight whenever a strike occurs. A dial on the reel gives the temperature at the depth being fished.

To use this instrument, you let out lure or bait on 20 feet or more of line. The line at that point is clipped to the snap release on the weight. Both line and weight then are lowered (while you pay out line from your rod and reel) until the dial on the device (activated by a temperature probe

The Lowrance LTG 200 Fish-N-Temp Rig records temperature and depth at which lure is trolled, releases line when a strike occurs.

on the weight) records the temperature of the water in which you want to troll. Adjustments in depth can be made at will to keep the weight (and the fishing line and lure trailing from it) at the desired level. A strike on the lure pulls the line from the snap release, thus freeing it from the weight and allowing you to handle your fish on just rod and reel.

Sometimes it is necessary to troll at great depth to reach the proper temperature level preferred by the fish. Heretofore anglers have had to estimate depth, but the LTG 200 registers temperature and depth, so adjustments can be made when necessary, with all guesswork eliminated.

Electronic depth-probing instruments are helpful for trolling accurately at mid-depths. For example, let's say that the temperature probe says the correct depth is twenty-three feet and we want to be sure the bait or lure trolls at that depth. Using the depth probe, we find an area of that depth. We let out a sinking line until the lure bounces bottom. With that length of line out, at that water speed, we are trolling at correct depth. We may need to take in a few feet to prevent the lure from catching on bottom, but we remember the old maxim that we aren't trolling deep enough along the bottom if the lure doesn't snag or touch from time to time.

Another of the instrument's advantages is that it tells us when to take in line to avoid snagging. If, for example, we are trolling at twenty-three feet and the instrument suddenly registers a decrease in depth, we would take in line to clear bottom. Then, based on a reading of our hydrographic (depth contour) map, we would change course to return to the proper depth.

A REVIEW OF DEEP STRUCTURE FISHING

The following five points summarize the procedure for finding fish in deep water.

1. Knowing the preferred water temperature of the fish we want to catch, we find the depth at which this temperature occurs. An electronic temperature probe is the most accurate method for determining this depth.

2. Use a hydrographic (depth contour) map to chart the path of ideal trolling or to mark the bottom structures at that depth which are presumed hot spots.

In doing these two things we have immediately eliminated at least 90 percent of the lake, so we don't need to waste time with it. We will confine our fishing to a definite depth, and to only a few places (or a trolling path) at that depth.

In selecting bottom structure let's also remember that it may contain *substructure*, which narrows down the presumed hot spots even more. What is substructure? It is the best part of the structure. Three examples: If the structure is a submerged stream bed, its substructure would be the sharp bends in it, and particularly the deeper outside curve of the bends. If the structure is a mass of standing dead timber or heavy brush, its substructure would be open places in it. If the structure is a submerged roadbed, its substructure would be the ditches beside it.

Tackle shops should have maps of regional waters, or should know where to obtain them.

3. Fish the selected structures only long enough to determine their productiveness, because fish from time to time prefer one type of structure to another. If a structure is unproductive, don't waste time with it.

Some structures may be unsuitable for fish because of oxygen deficiency —for example, the lower level of a stratified lake. In oxygen-deficient areas there may be places where there is an oxygen inversion—an area in the deficient part which contains sufficient oxygen. Electronic probes are available to measure oxygen levels at any depth, but they are usually used only by professionals. The probe measures the parts per million of oxygen dissolved in water. Between six and twelve PPM is ideal, but some species can tolerate a little more or less.

4. In fishing selected structures, many anglers like to use three rods. One may be rigged with a weighted plastic worm, one with a deep-running plug, and one with a Johnson weedless spoon, probably with a pork rind, part of a plastic worm, or some other flutterer attached. Everyone has his preferences. Try three or four casts with each lure. If nothing happens, move to another structure. If something does happen, find out what type of lure is the best taker, and stick with it. These recommendations are primarily for bass in deep structures.

5. When a good structure is found, concentrate on others that are similar. For example, if the fish are in curves in a submerged stream bed or in open spots in masses of standing timber, concentrate on these to the exclusion of other places. The fish are following a *pattern*—a similar environment of temperature, oxygen, cover and food, and we should fish the pattern. Some patterns may be productive for several days. When they cease producing, we must start over.

Two other points might be added with reference to stillfishing in a lake. An electric motor won't spook fish, at least for very long. Anchors for both bow and stern keep the boat in position for proper coverage of the area. It can't be done properly if the boat is allowed to swing. Lower anchors quetly and avoid noise in the boat. Noise can turn a hot spot into an unproductive one.

Structure fishing is a bonus of the electronic age, but even experts admit that it isn't easy. After rereading and absorbing the information in this book, you must apply the knowledge to specific situations. It takes time and thought and planning. You may have to try several structures before finding a pattern that pays off. But when it does, it pays off in spades!

6

Tips on Trout – From Top to Bottom

SPRING TROUT FISHING—STREAMS

In earlier days. at the start of the New England trout season, I would be up before dawn to be rigged and ready to go at first light. I don't do it any more because it doesn't make much sense. The fact that it's uncomfortably cold and that mush-ice clogs rod guides isn't the main point. The point is that fishing is better in the afternoon when waters get a bit warmer. On a sunny early-season day, water temperatures can rise 15 degrees between sunup and mid-afternoon, and this can make a big difference in the fishing.

Those who want to venture forth when water temperatures are 50 degrees or less are advised to use bait. Bright red garden worms, cleansed of their loam by a day or so in damp moss, more wiggly and less slimy then, are the favorite bait for frigid streams. Hellgrammites, crayfish, grubs, if you can find them, also produce. Add a split shot or two to get them down, if necessary, because the bait should be rolled along the bottom. Some fishermen prefer big nightcrawlers at such times, perhaps on the theory that, if a small worm is good, a bigger one is better. I don't think this is so. Trout adapt their body temperature to that of the surrounding water. When it's cold their metabolism is very low. They hug bottom; won't move to any extent to take food; need very little, and prefer smaller baits to bigger ones.

Many of us don't enjoy baitfishing for trout, but it seems to be the best answer in cold weather. Those who want to use flies early in the season can try nymphs, small streamers or bucktails, fished slowly on the bottom. Small spinners or wobblers, worked as slowly as possible along the bottom, also are second best bets. I know fishermen who "sweeten" their streamers or hardware by adding a piece of worm to the hook. If it's fresh it may add the enticement of scent.

Another aversion of mine is to fish for freshly stocked hatchery trout, most of which are dumped into streams in early season to make fishermen feel their licenses are good investments. Tame trout expect to be fed, and will take almost anything that moves. A fisherman phoned one day to report taking his limit in a few minutes. He theorized that, since hatchery trout were fed liver, they must have grown fond of it. So he obtained a piece of beef liver, cut it into small strips, and baited his hook by impaling the end of a strip on the barb. He said it had worms beaten seven ways to Sunday!

With that, let's let a few weeks pass and discuss trout fishing when the weather is more comfortable.

On a day later in spring we took water temperatures hourly while fishing with nymphs and small streamers. At nine o'clock the stream's temperature was 51 degrees, and was only a degree warmer at ten. Eleven o'clock had raised it 4 degrees to 55, and 3 more at noon to 58. The morning's fishing was poor; mostly small ones. By one o'clock the stream had warmed 2 more degrees to 60; then a big jump to 64 an hour later. This rise to ideal temperature levels brought a decided improvement in the fishing. Fish that had hugged bottom in the colder water now began to rise. The warmth brought on a small insect hatch, causing dimples and splashes in holding spots behind midstream rocks and along steep brushy banks. Conditions like this make flies and weighted lures superior to bait. One reason is that we can keep them fishing. Bait must be changed frequently. When we're fussing with bait we're taking time away from fishing!

Anglers who take stream temperatures can tell whether they should fish along the bottom or higher up. They can predict when trout should leave holding areas and travel to feeding ones such as riffles and the tails of pools. They can accurately guess what types of lures or flies to use.

We have discussed the holding spots of the three popular trout species, as well as the steelhead and cutthroat of western waters, in previous chapters. The pattern of brown trout differs slightly from that of the others. They can tolerate somewhat warmer water, up to 75 degrees or so, if it contains enough oxygen. They prefer places where they can remain hidden, such as the dark waters of undercut stream banks, culverts with moderate or slowly flowing water, and the sanctuaries provided by tree roots and log jams. Look for the big ones in the more inaccessible spots.

Brown trout are also fonder of night feeding than brookies and rainbows seem to be. Find a good brown trout pool and become familiar with it during daylight. Plan how you would fish the pool after dark. Then go there by moonlight and fish for the big ones, which should be venturing from their hideaways. Brown trout seem to lose much of their caution after dark, and they look for food by sound as well as by sight and scent. Frogs that make too much commotion don't last very long. Big floating flies and sinking streamers, slapped on the surface, may bring strikes.

Brown trout have a well-deserved reputation for being smart, and they are smart enough to know when they are safe. A stream flowing through a New York town maintains a protected area for them which doubles as a tourist attraction. People collect on the bridge to watch trophy tackle busters lying peacefully in plain sight in the shallow stream below. The fish lie in the shadow thrown by the bridge, many of them with their noses almost touching the line of sunlight. People feed them, but the town constable lingers nearby to be sure nothing is dropped that has a hook in it. Wherever fishing is allowed, don't neglect the shade under bridges!

Ponds and Lakes

Early in the season surface fishing is excellent when the ice melts, but only if it has been windy enough to mix the water. Trout and salmon are cold then, and search for relative warmth. Under such conditions we should find them in sunny, shallow water close to the shoreline, where they can find protection under tree roots and fallen timber.

When a good breeze is stirring on a warm day we know that it pushes warmer surface water to the windward shore, sort of piling it up there. The breeze also carries surface foods, so such an area should be productive.

When buds begin to pop in early spring the smelt in lakes, as well as some species of baitfish, collect in stream estuaries and move up the streams to spawn. Trout and landlocked salmon know this, and collect near the stream mouths. After spawning, the smelt and baitfish return to the lakes again, so stream mouths should offer excellent spring fishing as long as this period lasts.

The trick here is to anchor the boat about a hundred feet from the entering stream, over a channel or deep hole, if there is one. Use a streamer fly or bucktail that resembles the baitfish in size and color. Cast it far out on a sinking line, giving it plenty of time to sink deep. Then strip the fly in fast. As it nears the boat, change its action to sharp jerks. Fish may be following the fly and may take it only when it is given different action close to the boat. With this method, the area should be fan-casted, and this can be repeated for as long as is desired, because we are working on cruising fish. A fruitless cast to one spot doesn't mean there won't be a big trout or salmon there on the next cast.

In many places this kind of fishing is best as early as anglers can pry themselves out of bed. This may be because major baitfish runs happen during the night and just before sunrise, or because the gamefish feed more actively then.

Of course an alternative to casting is trolling; close to the surface when water temperatures are correct, but deeper when necessary. Fly-rodders use streamers or bucktails, let out fifty feet or so of sinking line, and give the fly, which is only slightly below the surface, a bucktailing action. If this doesn't work, they add a split shot or two to the leader butt. Color-coded lead-cored lines are the alternative for going deeper. Long, bright wobblers or small plugs are used for deep trolling.

After most of the baitfish have left the streams, schools may be found in the lake or traveling near shore. These schools are usually followed by the trout and landlocked salmon.

We said that streamers or bucktails should imitate prevalent baitfish in color, size and shape. Popular patterns, in the Northeast, at least, are smelt simulators such as Gray Ghost, Nine-Three, Black Ghost and Imperial Supervisor. Three other streamers, lesser known, are proven killers. Some readers may be interested in their dressings:

HERB JOHNSON SPECIAL

Head color: Silver paint, with yellow eye and black pupil. The head is
quite large. (Hook size: No. 2 or 4 streamer hook.)
Body: Black wool, fairly full.
Ribbing: Embossed flat silver tinsel (wound in reverse, toward tyer).
Throat: White bucktail, as long as the wing.
Wing: A very small bunch of bright yellow bucktail, slightly longer than
the hook; on each side of this two strands each of red and blue
fluorescent nylon floss; on each side above the floss one strand of Peacock herl; over this a rather sparse bunch of brown bucktail dyed
yellow. (All components are of the same length, slightly longer than
the hook. On a No. 2 long-shanked hook the dressing is 2¾ inches long.)

This fly, originated by Herb Johnson, of Portland, Maine, has been a
sensational producer for Atlantic salmon as well as for trout, landlocked
salmon and bass. We don't quite know why, but the fact remains!

SIDE-WINDER

Head color: Red
Body: Flat silver tinsel
Wing: A few hairs of white bucktail, over which are 2 red-brown very
narrow and fine furnace hackles, mounted low on sides, one side showing front of one hackle and the other side showing *back* of the other
one, both extending only to the bend of a long-shanked hook.

This simple streamer was originated by the Reverend Elmer James
Smith, of Prince William, New Brunswick. Its secret is its slimness. Presumably it imitates a spent smelt. It is an excellent trout taker anywhere.

KENNEBAGO SMELT

Head color: Black
Body: Flat silver tinsel
Ribbing: Twisted silver tinsel
Underbelly: White bucktail
Wing: Red and blue (mixed) bucktail, over which are 4 black saddle
hackles, topped with 6 strands of Peacock herl.
Throat: A small bunch of yellow hackle fibers.

This excellent smelt imitation was originated by Bud Wilcox, of
Rangeley, Maine. Bud is an excellent fly dresser who also originated the
Tri-Color, a streamer imitating a crayfish.

If action tapers off near stream mouths after sunup, look for nearby
coves where large rocks can be seen on the bottom. Try a flashy streamer
fly or weighted lure on a bright day, and a duller one on a dark day. Let
the streamer sink well down, and strip it in fast. This is best done from an
anchored or drifting boat; trolled flies may not get down between the
rocks, or may get hung up there.

In early spring we often find good evening fishing along rocky shorelines, especially on the windward side of the lake.

SUMMER TROUT FISHING—STREAMS

As surface waters grow warmer, to 65 degrees or more, the spring pattern changes to a more or less static one which lasts until the cold weather of fall. Let's see where to find fish under these circumstances.

Earlier in this book we compared deep streams, and particularly their pools, to tunnels where the fastest flow is in the center but is braked by obstructions along sides and bottom. This is true, to a lesser degree, of the surface. We observed that, except when surface feeding occurs, gamefish lie in protected places close to the sides and along the bottom, but they usually won't be found out in middle depth, where beginners so often fish for them. The importance of carrying a thermometer was stressed because we look for water temperatures of about 61 degrees for trout. If surface waters are in that range, fly fishing should be good on top, especially late in the afternoon, because most insect hatches occur when surface waters are just right for trout. If the surface water is much warmer or colder, we must fish close to bottom in protected places.

In going on from there let's start with a few general observations. When the air is colder than the water the fishing should be poor, and there should be no surface activity. Fog over the water usually indicates this. We have the choice of working the bottom or of waiting until the sun warms the air. This is also true of windy days, because there are fewer hatches then, and those that occur are driven from the stream.

Conversely, summer fishing should be good during or after a rain, particularly when the river is rising. While this may discolor the stream a bit, it also dislodges food, washing it downstream and putting trout on the feed. I remember many instances of this. My fishing companion dropped me off at a bridge one summer afternoon, telling me the car would be at another bridge about a mile and a half downstream. Soon after he left, a pelting rain began, but since there was no cover, I continued fishing. Nearly every time I cast the tiny streamer fly to a good-looking spot a trout took it. Many of them were surprisingly large. I switched to nymphs, with the same result. Fish were on the feed and took almost anything. I released all but two, which were enough for dinner. At dusk I arrived at the lower bridge and found my partner asleep in the car. He had done poorly because he hadn't wanted to get wet!

When streams are warm in summer, look for places that cool them, and carefully fish for trout there. Cold-water brooks are excellent places because trout collect at their mouths and they run up them in summer. If the bank is undercut where the brook enters the stream, the mouth is almost sure to be a hot spot. When the stream is too warm, try the brook itself.

Another sign of a hot spot is trickling cold water from a spring. Such trickles often come from a gravel bank, or as tiny brooklets flowing in. Look for protection where they enter the stream, or slightly downstream of it.

Anglers who watch water temperatures look for signs of feeding activity when these temperatures are optimum for trout. Part of their education is to sit quietly on a bank and to look into a pool to see what's going on. We may see the flashing bodies of feeding trout in head-down and tail-up stances as they root in the gravel of shallow pools. The trout are said to be "tailing," and they are picking nymphs from the bottom. There usually are no insect hatches at such times. This is the signal to fish with nymphs along the bottom. What kind of nymphs? We don't have to try to be scientific about it. Just turn over a few stones in the pool and see what's clinging to them. Imitate the biggest as closely as possible—or catch a trout and check its stomach contents. If it contains nymphs, bits of gravel, and detritus, the trout are bottom feeding, and we imitate the nymphs they have eaten with the closest artificial approximations in our fly book.

Another type of feeding activity is when we see the backs and tails of trout as they break the surface. In this case they are "nymphing"; taking emerging nymphs on or near the surface as they rise to hatch into flies. Sometimes a trout will jump as it tries to catch a fly which has emerged and starts to fly away. We then have at least three choices. We can use an artificial nymph, let it sink and slowly come to the surface. We can use a wet fly of the same type that is emerging and let it drift on or below the surface. We can use a dry fly and fish it dry or wet in the same manner.

A third type of feeding is when trout are "dimpling"; sucking in emerging insects. It may look as if these small dimples were made by small fish, but big ones break the surface film so slightly that the dimples they make are very tiny. This is the type of activity that calls for dry flies. If the artificial resembles whatever is hatching with reasonable accuracy, and if it doesn't get strikes, try a smaller fly of the same pattern rather than changing the pattern. If one chooses to vary from it, a lighter colored fly on a bright day, or a darker colored fly on a darker day should get results. We must see the fly to hook the fish, which may be difficult under some conditions. In such cases try a fly with some white on it, a Royal Coachman, or a bivisible with a white collar.

In general, when trout are feeding in these ways the fly fisherman does better than those who use hardware or bait. The fish are being selective, and we should try to imitate what they are feeding on. Many advanced books have been written on nymph and dry-fly fishing. They can be of great interest to anglers who want to specialize in these methods, but all this can become rather complicated. It's loads of fun, and it pays off, but casual anglers can do pretty well with the basics which have been discussed.

Ponds and Lakes

A knowledge of water temperatures is important in finding trout in ponds and lakes during the summer. We may see trout, or put lures near them, when temperatures are out of their range (perhaps because they can't find better ones), but they are much less inclined to take lures then. Shoal water is probably too warm, except perhaps early in the morning or late in the evening. Anglers who don't want to fish deep for trout in summer can often find them near the surface in cooler water—the mouths of cold-water brooks and spring holes.

When a fast inlet stream pours into a subsurface channel in a pond or lake the force of the flow may take its colder water through the warm upper layer down into the stratified thermocline level where water temperatures should be suitable for trout. This provides an escape route, or feeding route, from the depths of the pond or lake into the stream. Many trout frequent stream mouths anyway, so they should be good trouting spots in summer.

Anglers exploring stream mouths from boats might anchor or drift in area *B-B* to fish the visible stream mouth area *A-A*. When they do this they may catch only a few small trout, or none, because they are over the lip of the stream mouth where the larger trout usually lie. Since the fish almost surely have been disturbed, they probably won't take bait or lures.

I like to approach stream mouths from as near shore as possible, preferably by drifting with the breeze, holding the anchor overboard and ready. Avoid noise and motion. Sit there for ten minutes or so to look at the situation, at the same time giving the trout (which may have been disturbed somewhat) the feeling that all is well. How does the stream enter the lake, straight or in a curve? Do we see a sharp drop-off, or a deep channel? What are the good hiding places in moderate flow? Are there any signs of insect hatches or feeding activity? How should the casting sequence be planned? What is the near-surface temperature? Should we fish deep, or shallow? What lures or baits should be best? It pays to think things out. If I may substitute "anglers" for "angels," a classic line would read, "For fools rush in where anglers fear to tread." Many a fine fishing spot has been ruined temporarily by rushing in without prior planning!

When there is a drop-off in an entering stream the best fishing should be in the drop-off. Look for rises there. If none are seen, lures must be fished deep.

When a breeze is blowing toward an inlet stream it brings surface foods with it, particularly in summer. The breeze tends to push the foods into the stream mouth, but the stream's current tries to push them back. This causes the formation of a food line. When there is little wind the line may be scattered and fairly far out, but a stronger wind will compact it and drive it in toward the current. Beginners may not notice this because the line is often rather scummy, and we must look closely to see spent insects and terrestrials in it. If we do look closely we may see the dimples of feeding fish as they suck in these foods from below. In this case put on a dry or wet fly that approximates the majority of the food, cast it into or near the food line, and give it the slightest possible action to attract attention. A representation of a bee or a grasshopper is excellent.

Another very important type of hot spot in summer is the spring hole. Some of these are deep in pond or lake and can't be found except by luck with a depth thermometer. Once found, their locations should be marked carefully and kept secret, because in summer they will be good year after year.

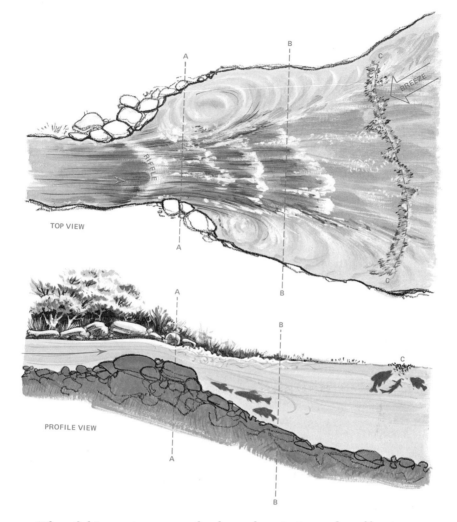

When fishing a stream mouth, shown here in top and profile views, stay well beyond line A-A in order to cast to the drop-off at B-B. If there is a breeze blowing toward the mouth, a food line (C-C) may form against the outflowing current where baitfish and gamefish gather, so anchor farther out and cast to the line.

Why keep them secret? I used to fish a wilderness trout lake in Maine which contained a large spring hole about fifty feet from shore in water nearly ten feet deep. Large trout collected in the hole and, usually being hungry, were quite easily caught. We fished for fun there, using barbless dry flies in the evening, and rarely killing a trout. But others learned about it, including an aircraft owner who flew in with friends as often as twice a day. They nearly always left with limits, or better, and the hole soon be-

This entering stream has a drop-off shelving deeply into the lake. The angler in the foreground is fishing it near the far edge, using a fast-sinking line. There is a minor feed line extending under his rod tip, as well as along the edge.

came fished out. The spot isn't much good any more, and only a few small trout remain in the lake.

I once visited another remote Maine lake where an old gentleman staying at the camp always left early in the morning in his canoe and returned fishless every evening. On the day before we were to go home he took me aside.

"You aren't the kind who kills too many trout," he said. "How would you like a couple of big ones to take home with you? If I show you where they are, will you agree never to tell anyone?"

Of course I agreed, and accompanied him in his canoe. He paddled into a cove dense with lily pads—more of a bassy place than a trouty one. He stopped the canoe among the pads while we watched a moose feeding nearby.

"See any trout?" he asked.

"There is a rise or two in that big opening in the pads," I answered. "They don't look very big."

He quietly paddled a little closer, until the canoe's bow was away from the pads.

"Put your fly in the center of the opening," he directed.

I laid it out, checked it slightly over the center, and let it flutter down. A trout took it instantly, and it was a big one.

"Not good enough," he said. "Let's let it go."

We had fabulous fishing there, breaking a few tippets when fish became tangled in the pads, but bringing many others to boat and releasing them. We each kept two trout of trophy size and started back for camp as a pair of loons called to each other, and black shadows from the forested hills helped patches of evening fog blanket the lake.

"Of course that was a spring hole; a real good one," he remarked as we came in sight of lights blinking on in the camp. "I didn't mean that you shouldn't bring anyone else to it, but please use good judgment. When a spot like that is overfished, the best fishing in this part of the lake is ruined. Most of the big trout come into spring holes in summer, and I don't know of any other here."

"I watched you return every night, and never saw you bring in a trout," I said. "I'll bet you hooked a lot of them!"

"Yes, a great many," he said softly. "But I only wanted a couple to take home. I didn't kill any others."

The old man and I swapped letters and flies for several years, but we never did meet again. One day the mail brought a beautiful Payne fly rod and a box of flies, including some well chewed ones I had sent him when new, long ago. With the gift was a note from his widow.

"He wanted you to have these," she wrote. "Please keep them fishing for him."

My introduction to spring holes happened in early youth when an older friend and I took a two-week canoe trip into what then was the wilderness of Maine. We carried in to a remote pond and fly fished the shoreline. By old standards the trout weren't very big, but some would be eye-poppers now. Finally, my companion laid a streamer close to shore and hooked a four-pounder. On the return trip he did it again. On the next trip down the shore he said, "I'll bet you a dollar I can take a trout of over two pounds on the next cast."

I lost the dollar.

"You've got a lot to learn about trout fishing," he said. "Don't you know I took each of those three trout from exactly the same spot, and don't you know why?"

I admitted ignorance.

"Look there," he pointed. "The bank is eroded, but you see a lush green spot, and water trickling down. It has made a hole at waterline as big as a bathtub. That's a spring hole, and big trout lie in there during warm weather. Put your fly there and see what happens."

I hooked a three-pounder.

That was my introduction to spring holes, and I never forgot it. I never was allowed to, because he has kidded me about it ever since!

When near-surface water isn't too warm for feeding activity on ponds and lakes, there are other visible manifestations of where to find fish in addition to the others already discussed. One of these is wind ripples, as shown in the photo on page 120.

Trout (and other fish) which are surface feeding lie below the edges of wind ripples for two reasons. The ripples (or "riffles," as they are some-times called) give trout more of a feeling of security than do the glassy parts of the lake's surface. When this picture was taken a large midge hatch was in progress. The newly hatched chironomids were piling up in windrows at the edge of the ripples, and trout were sucking them in. At

A ripple line on a lake is always a possible hot spot. Fish feel secure under the ripples, and hatching flies sometimes pile up at the edges.

other times slight breezes would blow other types of insects to such places.

This is another instance of where fly tackle should do better than other equipment. Use a floating line with a long, fine leader, a nymph imitating the midge pupa, or a dry fly suggesting the adult insect. Drop it at the edge of the ripple line.

Another place to find trout when there are no surface or visible subsurface indications of their presence is in a small pond with a weedy bottom. When the surface is very weedy, the trick is to fish open places amid the weeds.

Many lakes have no weeds or pads showing. Then you have to anchor at random and fan-cast the area with as long a line as possible. Use a sinking line and work a streamer fly just over the weeds. Give the cast time to sink, counting seconds. You'll bring back grass on some casts, but try to get as deep as possible without doing so. When the fly has had time to sink it should be stripped in fast.

I know of ponds like this in the Northeast where the bottom is so weed-covered that it looks like a dark green rug. All the weeds are about the same height, several feet below the surface. Other such places show more readable structure such as boulders, gravel bars, submerged tree trunks and submerged brush piles. If the lake contains trout, surface-feeding fish will frequently be observed dimpling, making head-and-tail rises, or swirling along the edges of wind riffles where floating food tends to collect.

When surface water is a bit too warm or cold for trout, they may feed on the surface anyway when a good hatch is in progress. When water is a bit too cold, peak feeding on sunny days should be around noon or early in the afternoon. When water is a bit too warm, the best fishing should be near evening when temperatures start to decline. On cloudy or rainy days, when the light is poor, fish will venture from hiding places more often, making feeding periods longer.

FALL TROUT FISHING—STREAMS

When stream temperatures descend toward the low 60's brook trout and brown trout (as well as landlocked salmon and some other species) move into stream outlets (often as far out as stream currents exist) to wait there until water temperature, volume of flow and the urgency to spawn impel them to swim upstream, sometimes far up into the gravel of small feeder brooks. In Maine's former wilderness I have parted streamside bushes after the fishing season closed in October and have seen so many brook trout lying over the gravel that nearly all of the stream's bottom was covered by them. Brown trout do this, too, spawning in some areas as late as February. Both species also will spawn in shallow gravel or rocky areas of lakes if satisfactory stream conditions do not exist.

Thus, in the fall, the places to fish are outlets of streams flowing into lakes. Look for fairly deep channels with moderate flow, particularly in the shade. Such places may be quite wide. Perhaps believing in the safety of numbers, the fish are less shy than usual, but they may not take lures as avidly as their urge to spawn increases.

This is a time to take trophy trout. Many big ones which now grace library walls were caught quite easily and without much skill because so many were concentrated near stream mouths or farther upstream in pools and runs. To avoid having too many taken, and thus to help preserve the fishery, many states close their trout seasons before spawning reaches its peak, but the legal week or two before this can provide fabulous fishing. In this age when trouting needs all the help it can get, anglers are urged to use restraint by fishing for fun and limiting the kill to a single trophy, if it is desired. Of course the trophy should be a male. Males are more colorful for mounting, and not as necessary for reproductive purposes because one can fertilize the eggs of several females.

Ponds and Lakes

When cold fall nights reduce surface temperatures of lakes the trout begin to roam more widely. The solutions to finding them depend on water temperatures and structure; this being stream mouths (which we have discussed), log jams, rocky coves, windward shores and other places which now should be familiar.

It pays off to be observant. One day a French-Canadian guide and I were fishing a remote lake in northern Quebec. In outboarding from one spot to another I noticed a shady cove filled with drifted logs, and called the guide's attention to it. He shook his head. "No fish there," he said.

After supper I took a canoe and went there alone. The water was clear and deep, and the setting sun threw shadows over the cove. I quietly drifted in until the canoe sidled up to a floating log, put a streamer fly into the air, and dropped it near a log. There was an immediate swirl, and a big trout had it. He bored down deeply. The trick of course was to try to get him away from the log jam, which I managed somehow or other by

TEMPERATURE-ACTIVITY TABLE FOR TROUT

AT WATER SURFACE TEMPERA- TURES	WATER IS	FISH ARE	FISHING SHOULD BE	FISH ARE FOUND	SUGGESTED LURES
FREEZING TO 40° F	MUCH TOO COLD	INACTIVE	VERY POOR	VERY DEEP (in lakes or pools)	BAIT FISHED DEEP
40°–50° F	TOO COLD	PASSIVE	FAIR	DEEP (Or along shorelines or riffles where winter is warmer)	LIVE BAIT SPOONS OR SPINNERS NYMPHS STREAMER FLIES
50°–60° F	JUST RIGHT	ACTIVE	GOOD	NEAR SURFACE	WET FLIES STREAMER FLIES NYMPHS SPOONS OR SPINNERS
60°–70° F	JUST RIGHT	VERY ACTIVE	EXCELLENT	NEAR SURFACE	DRY OR WET FLIES STREAMER FLIES NYMPHS SPOONS OR SPINNERS
70°–80° F	TOO WARM*	ACTIVE TO PASSIVE	FAIR	DEEP (Or in spring holes, brook mouths, shaded streams)	LIVE BAIT STREAMER FLIES NYMPHS SPOONS OR SPINNERS
80° F AND UP	MUCH TOO WARM	INACTIVE	VERY POOR	VERY DEEP (Or in spring holes and cold water brooks)	BAIT FISHED DEEP

OPTIMUM TEMPERATURES

TOLERANT TEMPERATURES

(Copyright 1949, 1971 and 1974 by Joseph D. Bates, Jr.)

While all anglers and scientists will not agree completely with these ranges, they are the most generally accepted.

* These ranges are more accurate for brook trout than for rainbow or brown trout which are active at temperatures about 5° higher than shown here.

backing the canoe with a paddle in one hand while holding the fly rod in the other.

Out in deeper water it was necessary to use all the power the leader's tip would stand to prevent the fish from snagging on dead branches which littered the bottom. The trout stayed near the surface and I finally netted him. He was a fat, humpbacked male brook trout weighing 6¼ pounds, brilliant in fall mating colors.

After gloating over this prize while I smoked a pipe I drifted in again and cast the same streamer to another log. A cast or two later hooked another male trout of almost the same size. I brought him to boat, bent the fly from his jaw, and watched him swim away, perhaps to give another angler a thrill at another time.

The trout saved was mounted by Herbie Welch, of Oquossoc, Maine, one of the greatest anglers and taxidermists of trout who ever lived. He looks down from the wall as I write this; a reminder that it pays to know how to "read the water" and to use one's own judgment. The spot may have been a spawning area. I don't know. By the time the second fish was released it was too dark to try any more, and the aircraft came in for us the next morning.

One of the highlights of a rather comprehensive fishing career happened in October of 1948 when the revered angler Joe Brooks, and I visited Lake Pend O'Reille, in Idaho. The lake was famous as the home of giant rainbow (Kamloops) trout. and I wanted to catch one. Local gossip was that the fish were still down deep because the lake remained stratified and hadn't "turned over" yet. My water temperature readings indicated that it had.

Up to that point the world's record (which still holds) was a thirty-seven pound rainbow caught on wire by trolling deep. That sort of thing doesn't interest me very much. I wanted one taken with light tackle on the surface.

After a day or two of scouting around and not catching anything very big, we decided to concentrate on the wide area of the mouth of the Clark's Fork River. Baitfish were there and temperatures were right. We were fishing from a launch; a wind was up, and I had to use spinning tackle which happened to have. a reel with 8-pound-test line. The lure was an oval wobbling spoon.

Nothing happened until midmorning, when the sun began to warm the surface water. Then, suddenly, the big trout struck. He went deep and stayed down. Since I had him in deep water it would be only a matter of time to raise him on a tightly bowed rod if the tackle held.

The fight wasn't very exciting. The trout would come up a bit and go down again, but he never showed until he was brought to the surface more than half an hour after being hooked. The net on board wasn't large enough to hold him, so Joe Brooks gaffed him for me. He weighed 31 pounds and 12 ounces, and would have gone a pound or two better if he could have been netted. He was a light-tackle record for many years.

The moral of the story, if there is one, is that anglers can read the lore in books such as this about how to find fish, but they must pause to think how to apply it to whatever situation arises—and every situation is a different one. In this case we spent several days doing what our hosts thought we should do before we applied logic to the problem. In the above two examples of catching a "big one" logic was applied which didn't happen to agree with local custom.

To avoid complication this chapter deals only with the more important species of what familiarly are called "trout." One important species, with habits somewhat different from the others, is the lake trout, sometimes referred to by other names such as Mackinaw trout or togue.

Since they are cold-water fish preferring temperatures between 40 and 45 degrees, lake trout are almost always found at these temperature depths in summer, with slight variations depending on longitude. These depths may be as much as a hundred feet. At these depths lake trout can be taken by bait (preferably live baitfish) or by jigging, but the best method is by trolling either with bait, wobbling spoons, or large bucktails back of spinners. This fishing is more for meat than for sport because fish brought up from such depths maintain little life.

When lakes "turn over" in spring and fall the situation is quite different. Then the trout come to the surface and into the shallows in search of baitfish. After heavy rains they often frequent the mouths of feeder streams, and sometimes go into the streams themselves.

Lake trout spawn in fall over gravel at their favorite temperature level. These places may be near shore, but they more often are on deeper structures farther out. Fishermen who locate appropriate structure at correct temperature depth can often fill the boat with lunkers.

Good fishing during and after the fall turnover period of lakes may last for several weeks until colder nights fill surfaces with ice and the stratification period begins. When that happens some northern fishermen get out warm clothes and ice-fishing equipment. Others dress flies, repair tackle, read angling books, and plan for the season to come. In other areas the fishing season never ends!

7

Scientific Bass Fishing

The dedication of trout fishermen in northern states is matched, if not surpassed, by bass enthusiasts to the south. If trout fishermen think theirs is a complicated sport they haven't seen the vast array of equipment used by chronic bass seekers, and the scientific ways in which they use it. Fast bass boats take them quickly wherever they want to go; they use noiseless electric motors guided by their feet to slowly prowl over deep structures pinpointed by electronic depth and temperature probing devices. The boats are equipped with everything needed for the comfort of fishermen, plus aerated and temperature-controlled wells to keep their catches healthily alive, probably for later release after having been counted in competitions. And then there is tackle; several rods for each angler so he can use different lures without wasting time to re-rig, plus boxes bulging with more lures and incidental equipment. Fishermen lacking this complex of gear can hire guides who have it, or they can make do with less. Bass fishing has reached the scientific age.

LARGEMOUTHS IN SHALLOW AREAS

Whether or not we have access to fancy boats and electronic gear we can wade the shallows to prospect for bass, or we can work along them while casting from a boat. We won't catch as many bass that way because they are either scattered or not there at all. Weedy, paddy and grassy shallows provide peak fishing when water temperatures reach the 60s in the spring and bass begin to spawn.

Bass spawn most often in April, in weedy sand or gravel areas only a few feet deep, usually quite near shore. They clean out roundish beds and make them slightly dish-shaped, depositing eggs near the centers. These beds are easily spotted, active ones being guarded by a bass. Of course there is a question of whether bass should be caught there, but some conservation authorities maintain it does no harm, and even may induce bigger fish in overpopulated waters. The bass merely act as guardians of the eggs, most of which will hatch anyway.

This is easy fishing because almost any lure, dragged slowly over a

Feeding area for largemouths—a shallow stretch near shore with plenty of vegetation. Dashed line shows the start of a drop-off, a perfect escape route into deep water.

bass bed, will be struck by the fish. He does this from anger, rather than from hunger, in order to get the intruder out of the way.

We know that feeding areas for largemouth bass include relatively shallow stretches, usually near shore, which contain an abundance of grasses, weeds, lily pads and other vegetation which usually grows above the water. These feeding areas have an escape or migratory route to deeper water, such as a deep drop-off nearby. In the photo there is a grassy but narrow shoreline also containing logs and brush; ideal bass habitat. The dashed line A outlines a drop-off from the shallow food shelf to a depth approaching twenty feet. The water over the shelf ranges in depth from two to ten feet. This type of spot can also be a spawning area. Other feeding areas may be vast expanses of lily pads, water hyacinths or stump ranches.

In shallow, weedy lakes with little deep water, bass don't need escape routes. In the photo taken on a lake in the Everglades of Florida, the angler is casting a weedless lure down a boat trail. Such shallow, open areas are often avenues of travel for bass and are likely to be slightly deeper than surrounding waters. The angler is being poled toward the wide area at the visible end of the boat trail. The edges should provide excellent fishing because bass lie in safety amid the thick grasses, facing toward open water, ready to flash out and pounce on anything swimming there.

In lakes with deep water bass spend most of their time in the structures we have described. They usually leave them near dusk for shallow feeding areas and remain there until the sun and warming water induce them to return the next morning—early if the sun is bright and later if it isn't. In deep water they seek a hard rather than a muddy bottom—a difference that can be registered by electronic probes even at considerable depths.

Fishing a boat trail in a Florida lake. These openings among the weeds are often travel routes for bass; the water is usually deeper than in the weedy areas.

Charles F. Waterman

An important fishing fact is that bass shun sunlight. Bright light dazzles them because, like most fish, they have no eyelids and their pupils can't expand and contract to protect their eyes from glare. Otherwise there would be no reason, beyond seeking suitable water temperatures, for leaving their feeding areas at all. As it is, they are driven from them to deeper structures to escape sunlight.

This provides a few hints for finding bass in shallow-water feeding areas. Don't look for them when the sun is bright, but they may linger longer in the shallows on dark days. When the sun is out and we want to fish the shallows, the best fishing will be in the shade; on the eastern sides of lakes in early morning and on the western sides in the afternoon.

The relative turbidity of water also should be considered. Some shore areas are very discolored by decomposition of vegetation and perhaps by run-off water. Bass stay in such places longer, and may remain in relatively shallow potholes more or less permanently. They also may remain in areas dense with large lily pads, which act as umbrellas to shade them from sun.

Experts maintain that when anglers face shallow water to fish for bass ninety percent of the fish are behind them—that is, in deeper structures. Also bass in the shallows are scattered rather than concentrated in schools of similarly sized fish in the productive "honey holes" so often found by people who understand structure fishing.

While this may be so, many anglers prefer fishing the shallows because of the challenge of casting accurately into openings in the weeds or along

127

their edges. They prefer the thrill of seeing a big bass smash a lure on top to the tamer experience of the deep strike. They often prefer to wade, and find it comfortable in warm weather to do so unencumbered by waders. They know that wading anglers can get closer to bass without spooking them than can those fishing from boats. When weed lines are deep, wading anglers can use innertube harness floats to drift into areas that are over their heads.

Shallow-water fishing is best in spring when waters are cool and bass are spawning. Productive lures are surface and shallow-running plugs, spinner baits and weedless plastic worms. Later spring calls for deep-water lures: plastic worms inched along the bottom, jig and eel combinations, and spinner baits fished slowly. Jigs with pork-rind eels attached are usually recovered with sweeping and twitching motions of the rod tip. Spinner baits (often called "safety-pin" lures) do best in shallow water when repeatedly allowed to flutter down on a nearly slack line and then jerked up. Thick cover along banks (including entering streams and ditches), drop-offs around islands, points of land, and the backs of coves amid cover are usually productive then. In summer bass are usually in deep holes and other deep structures during daylight, but also may be found in shallow springs and cold-water feeders. In the fall bass return to the flats more

This hot spot for bass is a hyacinth-choked creek mouth in a Florida lake. Note the current where the angler is fishing.

Charles F. Waterman

often, and cloudy midday fishing should be good, especially in shallows near deep water.

Many of us who prefer to hook bass on top like to do it with sturdy fly rods. Streamer flies do well, particularly colorful and floppy ones. These can be made weedless by dressing the hook with a loop of strong monofilament edging bend and barb, or by using flies dressed on Keel Hooks (made by Wright & McGill Company, of Denver, Colorado). Keel Flies are available in a wide variety of patterns. The fun here is to cast over pads or amid weeds, stumpage or brush and to drag the fly through. As it slithers into open stretches, a bass often takes it explosively. Leaders should test at least ten pounds, and perhaps as much as twenty or so because, once hooked, the fish must be kept on top and skidded in over the surface to open water in an effort to avoid tangles. (See Chapter 9 for details on lures.)

THE INFLUENCE OF WATER TURBIDITY

Discolored water is a boon to bass in deep water as well as shallow because it helps to protect them from glare while providing a partial sense of security. Some anglers feel that turbidity is more important to bass than temperature. Few lakes are so crystal-clear that we can see down twenty feet or more to bottom, and these rarely are good for largemouth bass. Bass lakes are always discolored to an extent—some very much so—by mineral or vegetable particles.

Fishermen who pay attention to turbidity think that bass lie over or in cover at depths where sunlight is minimal. They have ways of testing such depths, such as by lowering a white ceramic mug or a big, white sinking plug on a cord marked in feet. When the object is so deep it can't be seen, they think bass should be at that level or just below it. This may or may not be solid bottom, since bass like to lie near ledges or drop-offs. Regardless of turbidity, fishing on or over good structure is important.

In murky depths bass may not see lures well at a distance, so use bright ones—silver spoons, for example—which reflect whatever light there it. Also effective are lures that emanate sound or vibration, such as sonic plugs, or lures with spinners or rattles. Burke Fishing Lures, for example, sells a Rattllure, a short, bullet-shaped hollow weight with loose metal inside that rattles on the retrieve. This is strung over a plastic worm to provide both weight and sound. We know that bass zero in on objects which make sound, even if they can't see them, when the sound isn't an alarming one. Similarly, they zero in on lures which provide attractive scent, either natural baits or artificials. Because of this, many plastic worms and some other plastic lures are scented. Some of the scents, such as strawberry, seem rather far out, but evidently bass aren't very particular. A favorite scent is anise. It can be obtained at drug stores.

STRUCTURE VERSUS TEMPERATURE

In Chapter 5 I recommended that you should first determine the depth of ideal temperature and then locate structures at that depth. The great majority of anglers agree with this, but some do not. Those who don't think that bass acclimate themselves to a very wide temperature range and therefore that structure is of primary importance. This may be so in the South where lakes may not be very deep and water temperatures don't vary to the extent they do father north. When good-looking structure is found it may be worth while to fish it, even if the temperature there is a bit out of the optimum range. Generally, however, the procedure outlined should be followed.

This chapter discusses largemouth bass primarily in shallow water because locating largemouths in deeper water is a matter of structure fishing, and we have discussed structures in Chapter 5. All of them should be excellent for largemouths at one time or another. Most, but not all, of the structures should also be havens for other species, as we shall see.

SMALLMOUTH BASS

Daintier, smaller, fussier and more of a gourmet than the largemouth, the smallmouth bass gets many votes in the "scrappiest, pound for pound" category. The two species are similar in appearance, but the jaws of the smallmouth do not extend beyond a line perpendicular to the eye; the largemouth's do.

Although the two bass have many similarities, it is the differences that are important. Both species follow similar migratory routes from feeding shallows to cooler and deeper sanctuaries, but many smallmouths, because they have smaller appetites, remain in the depths year-round, and especially during the warmth of the summer. Both shun bright light, which makes their dusk to dawn feeding habits similar when they migrate to the shallows. Both spawn in shallow water near shore, but smallmouths make smaller and neater nests. Smallmouths—especially the bigger ones—spawn around exposed islands and on or near submerged ones.

Spawning takes place between late April and late June, depending on the region, when water temperatures reach about 60 degrees. Many lakes contain more fish than the food supply can support, so fishing over spawning beds may be allowed. There is usually a catch limit, a restriction to lures with single hooks, and most of the fish are released. Like largemouths, smallmouths on spawning beds will strike at almost anything. This is a good time for fly fishing, and conservation-minded anglers remove or bend down the barbs on hooks. On tight lines, very few fish get away until released.

Smallmouths are fussier than largemouths about water temperatures; only a few degrees makes a difference in their habitats or cruising levels. Optimum temperatures are between 59 and 65 degrees in northern regions and between 60 and 72 degrees in the South.

In Lakes

In deep water, which means about thirty feet, depending on temperature and clarity, smallmouths are found over rocky or gravel bottoms, usually where there is little or no vegetation. A favorite spot is a rock face, or rocky cliff, with boulders strewn on the bottom. Sometimes waterlogged timber clutters such places, but the fish cruise in plain sight, ignoring anglers peering down from boats above, evidently feeling safe in the security of depth and quick access to rocky hideaways.

Rocky drop-offs are equally good, as well as rocky or gravel points of land. Rocky islands and submerged mounds are excellent when anglers fish their lures at proper temperature depths. Submerged ledges also should pay off.

Proper fishing depth is a combination of optimum temperatures and light penetration, which is influenced by the relative turbidity of water. When it's clear, fish deep; when it's turbid, fish shallow. Fish may be at their higher optimum levels when the surface is disturbed by wind, but they will be much deeper when the surface is glassy—or will seek the shade of rocks and debris.

Smallmouth bass, like largemouths, migrate from the depths of lakes to shallow feeding areas, particularly between dusk and daylight. Crayfish, when present, are their favorite food, but they often dash out from schools to snatch small baitfish. In gravel areas they nose the bottom in search of crayfish and nymphs. When hatches are on they feed like trout, taking emerging mayflies, stoneflies and caddis flies on the surface. They also feed on worms, nightcrawlers, hellgrammites and small frogs. Smallmouths feed on the surface when water temperatures reach about 65 degrees.

In the Thousand Islands area of the St. Lawrence River fishermen habitually catch smallmouths on bait. They use spinning or spincasting tackle with a two-inch live batifish hooked under the dorsal fin or upward through the lips and a weight a foot or so above the bait to take it down. They cast this rig over weedy and sandy flats in relatively shallow water, leaving it on the bottom until a smallmouth picks it up.

ISLAND IN A RIVER

Anglers fishing in streams for trout sometimes hook smallmouth bass in spots that are marginally slow for the former but just right for the latter. This photo shows such a place. The land in the foreground is an island in a river whose two parts rejoin at the riffle (A). Since current in the foreground is minimal, trout fishermen should do better on the other side.

A few well-placed casts toward the brush on the far bank could hook a fish. The brush conceals undercut banks offering excellent protection for trout and especially smallmouth bass. While there is insufficient flow for a feed lane, insects will be dropping from the bushes, and the gravel bottom should be rich in nymphs and probably crayfish. Schools of minnows should be cruising and feeding in this pool, particularly along its deeper part close to the bushes, where fish symbols indicate the best water. The pool is too slow for rainbow trout and almost so for brownies and brook trout. However, a few lunkers can inhabit spots like this and remain undisturbed during their lifetimes.

When taking this picture we noted several schools of smallmouth bass cruising near the bushes and grubbing among the gravel for nymphs. While artificial nymphs might do well, buoyant dry flies such as Wulff patterns or flies with clipped deer-hair bodies should be most productive. Small streamers should also do well in color schemes corresponding to prevalent baitfish.

SMALLMOUTH POOL

This picture shows an ideal smallmouth bass pool, which should also contain some of the largest trout in the river. The boulder-choked hole is about ten feet deep, and one of the rocks is as big as an automobile. The main body of current swings away from the camera to the left. To the right, behind the overhanging rock ledge, it swings into a massive eddy. Smallmouth bass, and trout, too, seek relief from summer heat in deep pools like this. Seekers of smallmouths should mark this picture down in memory because it is rather typical of deep pools in rivers everywhere which are ideal for this species.

Since fish will usually be cruising deep, it seems best for fly fishermen to use fast-sinking shooting-head lines to work artificial nymphs or streamers down deep between the rocks. In such places I have found that one of the luckiest sinking flies is a small black marabou streamer with a silver tinsel body. An added bit of fluorescence, such as a tiny butt, also helps.

Anglers with spinning tackle should work small spinners and wobblers very deep. The large rocks reduce the danger of hang-ups, but this is a risk that should be taken. Try small spinner-and-fly combinations for smallmouths. Small, sonic fish-shaped plugs should do well, particularly when the sun is off the water, and they should be even more effective near darkness. Other suggestions: small, weighted plastic worms about three inches long, fished slowly, and small bucktail jigs. Like the fly mentioned above, a popular dressing for a jig for smallmouths is black marabou. These often do even better when an inch or so of plastic worm is put on the barb. We don't know what smallmouths think this represents, but they like it.

LARGE RIVER POOL

Here is another smallmouth bass lair in a big river. Because the current is wide, deep and slow, fish may be anywhere in the pool. It's a good spot for big brown trout, too, and steelhead would be holding here if they were in the river. Look for smallmouths on the inside of each edge. Big rocks, indicated by surface swirls, shouldn't be neglected.

The water here varies in depth between six and ten feet. The bottom is covered with irregular boulders of the type visible along the shoreline. Schools of baitfish seek shelter in the cover provided by the rocks, and crayfish are abundant here.

This is difficult water for fly fishing but it can be handled like the previous pool—with sinking lines and nymphs or streamers. On summer evenings when water temperatures are right, insect hatches may trigger surface feeding. Then, clipped deer-hair flies and bugs should bring strikes, as well as Wulff patterns, in sizes 4 to 8. Some authorities recommend cork poppers, worked slowly; others contend that noisy surface lures usually frighten smallmouths.

What are the best smallmouth spots on smaller streams? The deep inside bends where the current is slow, spring holes in summer, near sunken logs, beside and in back of boulders in slow water, the edges of food lanes in the deeper ends of pools, near the edges of sloughs, backwaters and eddies, and the mouths of incoming streams, especially in the spring.

Tallies kept by smallmouth fly fishermen indicate that wet flies (especially streamer flies) and spinner and wet fly combinations are favorite producers in the spring. This also is true in fall, with hair bugs added to the list. In early summer they favor small spinner and streamer combinations, small streamer flies, wet flies and hair bugs. The list for late summer is hair bugs, streamers and tiny plugs. Note that small streamers are favorites all the time. Fishermen agree that they're more effective than bait. Favorite streamer patterns include the Muddler Minnow, Wooly Worm, Mickey Finn and marabou patterns, black usually being considered the best.

While lures will be discussed in detail in Chapter 11, this might be a good place to comment briefly on fishing the popular clipped hair bugs, which are so effective all season when smallmouths are surface feeding (except in early spring). Let the bug lie motionless until all ripples it makes have disappeared. Then give it a series of very gentle twitches. Bass bugs can't be fished too slowly. Keep the rod tip close to the water and take in all slack line. When a bass comes up and takes the lure, strike it *hard*.

STRIPED BASS

Even though schools of striped bass enter coastal rivers (such as the Hudson, Sacramento and San Joaquin) to spawn, and smaller ones often remain year-round, the striper until recent years has been considered a saltwater fish. But stripers have been introduced in some large lakes and impoundments, and they have thrived and multiplied. Not as big as their saltwater cousins, which occasionally weigh sixty pounds or more, freshwater stripers are formidable adversaries on rod and reel, some weighing in at thirty pounds.

The striped bass is called a "rockfish" or "rock" in southern areas because its habitat is rocky waters. In the Northeast it has been nicknamed "linesides" due to the eight or so dark longitudinal stripes along its greenish to blackish back and silver sides.

Stripers migrate from lakes up rivers to spawn between April and July, depending on region, when water temperatures are in the 60- to 67-degree range. They spawn amid boulders and gravel.

Except in spring and fall the freshwater striper is a deep-water fish although schools may come to the surface in summer in certain areas to feed. When fish aren't showing on top we follow the now-familiar pattern of fishing rocky structures at the striper's favorite temperature depth. While this may vary somewhat between southern and northern latitudes, it generally is in the vicinity of 63 degrees.

To fish deep for stripers, anglers use the same methods as for lake trout: trolling, jigging or plugging at the correct temperature level along rocky shores, drop-offs and submerged structures, including brush piles. They use plugs, spoons and spinner-and-worm combinations. Stationary fishing calls for dressed or undressed jigs, jig and eel combinations, or live bait such as gizzard shad. Although usually hungry, striped bass can be temperamental at times, so we may have to experiment. Vertical jigging from a drifting boat is a favorite method from spring through fall.

When stripers are feeding on baitfish near the surface, usually in spring and fall when surface water temperature is right, schools can often be located by observing birds diving to feed on the baitfish themselves. Be ready for action with at least two rods rigged; perhaps one with a surface-popping plug and another with a metal jig like a Hopkins. Since running a boat into the school will put it down, circle it close enough to cast into the edge. If one lure doesn't bring a smashing strike, drop that rod and use the other. There isn't time to rerig, the school will stay near surface only for a few minutes, rarely as long as half an hour. Don't depend entirely on birds to find schools for you. Look for surface commotion.

Spinning or plugcasting tackle, with lines in the 10- to 15-pound-test range, is ideal for this kind of fishing. Lures between 1 and 1½ ounces are needed to get good distance on casts. Fly rods are very sporty but take too much time getting the line out, and winds may make long casts impossible.

In the spring look for striper schools migrating into river mouths and up the rivers. This is the ideal time for light-tackle angling. Stripers, like largemouths, come into the shallows to feed near dusk and during the night. Try fishing for them on moonlit nights when the fish can be heard, and their swirls can be seen as they feed. Wade, if possible, and for the best sport, use a fly rod. Spinning, spincasting or plugcasting tackle is useful, with lines in the ten-pound range, or even lighter in unobstructed water. Surface popping plugs and wigglers—Rapalas, Mirro-lures or their imitations—are productive. Fish them slowly, the poppers with a jerky action, the swimmers with a steady retrieve.

WHITE BASS

The striped bass and the white bass are thought to have originally been the same species, the white bass having become landlocked in ages past like the lake salmon. In southern lakes I have seen schools of them flurry to the surface like stripers. At other times we have drifted in shallow, gravelly coves and have seen schools of small white bass swimming there. They are fun to fish for because they are finical feeders, swimming behind a lure and carefully inspecting it before they strike. A slight change of action often induces them to take. These little cove fish rarely weigh as much as a pound, so tiny tackle is in order.

8

How to Locate Other Species

While those who prefer trout and bass fishing comprise a major part of the angling fraternity, a sizable segment are equally enthusiastic about the colorful and delicious panfishes, or the vicious-looking members of the pike family. Fishermen who specialize in these species need no hints on how and where to find them, but newcomers will save time and enjoy better catches by learning their habits and the types of structures they prefer. Scientific advances in the angling arts help to make this easier. Let's first discuss two of the principal panfishes—the crappie, or calico bass, and the bluegill, or bream.

CRAPPIES

There are two species of crappie, the black and the white, but the differences between them are so slight that they can be discussed as a single species.

In the spring—earlier in the South and later in the North—the secret of finding crappies is to locate their spawning areas. These are in rooty or weedy shallows, usually near shore, in water between one and ten feet deep. The best shallows are near drop-offs providing escape to deeper water, where the fish go after spawning.

Before spawning, crappies school in the drop-offs near the shallows, and they remain nearby for a week or two after spawning, so fishing in the shallows and along the drop-offs may be good for a month or more in spring. In deep lakes the fish never go very deep, preferring depths where the temperature is about 70 degrees. The best fishing is usually in spawning shallows on the windward shore where winds have driven surface food.

After spawning, loose schools of crappies go to deeper water where there is protective cover, submerged brush piles, stumps and dead trees, and deep channels. Or they seek shade near rocks, bridge abutments and docks. Impoundments, particularly in southern states, often provide abundant patches of brush piles, their tops usually showing above water. These usually are hot spots, and the biggest fish roam their centers. Thus, lures must be fished into the brush. This isn't as difficult as it might seem, but it does suggest taking along plenty of lures! In southern areas water temperatures aren't very critical in shallow lakes because surface and bottom temperatures vary very little and the fish are on or near bottom there. Crappies also seek deeper holes with sand or gravel bottoms. Like bass, they seem to shun muddy bottoms.

As spring progresses and warmer weather arrives, crappies, like bass, seek deeper water during the day and may come into the shallows to feed toward dusk. Unlike bass, they do not prefer weed beds, lily pads or grassy areas, but they do come into other structures which have been mentioned.

The traditional way of fishing for crappies was with a cane pole and a small, live minnow on a thin-wire hook suspended from a bobber to keep it at the desired depth. Nowadays a crappie pole is apt to be of telescopic fiberglass, about sixteen feet long, reelless, with a line a bit shorter than the pole itself testing between six and eight pounds. The bait is usually "dapped"—that is, dropped into likely-looking spots by raising and lowering the long pole.

Actually, artificial lures, if fished correctly, are superior to bait. One of the best is a weedless, weighted plastic worm, cast into brush and worked slowly through it. Another good one is a light-colored bucktail jig weighing between $\frac{1}{32}$ and $\frac{1}{4}$ ounce. This can be cast over spawning areas or into brush piles or other bottom structure and jigged out slowly. Since the single hook rides upward, a jig doesn't hang up often. When crappies are lying along drop-offs, they can be located by slowly trolling a jig, or perhaps two in tandem. You may have to try different depths to locate the strike zone.

The safety-pin lure is especially effective for crappies. It is available in various types and sizes, and many anglers consider it the best of all. It looks like an opened safety pin fastened to the line at its crotch. One prong is affixed to a spinner, the other to a jig (often with a hula-type skirt) or a baitfish representation on a weedless hook. The technique is to cast it out and let it sink, then jig it slowly up and down during the retrieve. It can also be trolled slowly.

Small weighted spinners are popular here and there, but they are inclined to snag. Since they must be fished slowly, the blade may not revolve. Pork-rind strips are also good crappie lures. Light-colored artificials imitating beetles, grubs and minnows, on No. 10 to 6 hooks, with or without small beads and a spinner, often produce. A split shot or two may be needed a foot or so above the lure.

BLUEGILLS

Usually called bream (pronounced "brim") in the South, the tasty, colorful and spunky bluegill is often underrated by anglers who have only hooked small ones in shallow water.

Bluegills are found in brush piles, flooded dead timber and other structures, but, unlike crappies, they are found near or in weed beds, lily pads and grassy areas. Look for them also near drop-offs of shallows with cover, off grassy points of land, and in stream channels.

Also unlike crappies, bluegills rarely take minnows, although they do consume tiny fry, often of their own kind. Their diet includes insects, crickets, grasshoppers and shrimp. Catalpa worms are a favorite bait for them in the South, and garden worms in the North.

In addition to these baits, bluegills when feeding near the surface take deer-hair bugs, sponge-rubber or chenille spiders and tiny poppers. When they're deep, bluegills hit wet flies (such as small Muddler Minnows) and tiny jigs, which should be slow sinkers, perhaps sweetened with a small piece of worm.

Small bluegills build nests in spring in shallow water. The bigger ones make them deeper, usually between five and ten feet, along sandy or gravel shorelines or on shallow reefs. Like bass, they often come into the shallows at dusk to feed, and they retire to the depths when near-surface water is too warm during the day.

Bluegills are very fussy about temperature, preferring water about 73 degrees. Thus we must experiment with depth, perhaps starting at four or five feet and going deeper until the strike zone is located. If we catch small ones, we move to a different spot. When we take a big one, we can assume that others should be nearby.

Floats are recommended to keep lures at proper depth and to signal light strikes. When the motion of the bobber indicates a strike the fish must be hooked instantly, before it has time to expel the lure.

After experimenting with various types of bobbers, my favorite is one of sponge plastic that can be strung on line or leader and held in position by a peg. These are about a half inch in diameter and can be cast with a fly rod. Try a weighted wet fly or a tiny marabou jig. If the lure isn't taken as it sinks, leave it alone for half a minute or so and then twitch it slightly. Grubs and other small baits, including garden worms, can be used on lures or on bare hooks. Experiment with lures, depths and locations; with the right combination you'll take a big bluegill on almost every cast.

YELLOW PERCH

In the early spring when the water exceeds 45 degrees, yellow perch migrate from lakes and ponds up feeder streams to spawn. In some rivers the size of the runs is amazing. Anglers can fill their freezers with tasty fillets by casting small spoons, spinners, jigs or streamer flies in baitfish colors. Since perch seem to like lures with a bit of yellow in them, a popular bucktail is one with a silver tinsel body and a wing of peacock herl over yellow over white, perhaps with a red throat.

After spawning time, look for perch in shallow coves and over reefs having sandy bottoms with patches of vegetation. They may also be in the shade of breakwaters and docks. Their favorite water temperature is in the 68-degree range, which is often not over ten feet in depth—although in mid-summer they may be much deeper. Serious perch fishermen use a temperature probe to find the correct depth and a contour map to find reefs or mounds at that depth. These may be far out in the lake.

Baits for perch include worms, crickets, grasshoppers, crayfish, grubs and insects, but their favorite is baitfish about two inches long. The usual practice is to first troll a minnow (hooked upward through the lips) under a bobber with a split shot or two on the line a foot or so above the bait to keep it down. When someone hooks a large perch the anchor is lowered and trolling gives way to casting. The same rig can still be used, but the minnow should be hooked under the dorsal fin.

Yellow perch are daytime feeders and will take baits or lures at any time, but the hours between noon and darkness seem to be best. Since the fish are notorious bait stealers, it is important to know when to set the hook. On taking the bait, the fish will run with it a short distance, turn it and swallow it head first. After allowing the fish to do this, the strike must not be delayed. This is a trick learned by experience. Fishermen who don't learn it easily prefer lures. Fly-rodders use a sinking line and a streamer or bucktail, in size 2 or 4.

PICKEREL

This smallest member of the pike family is called the "chain pickerel" because of its chainlike markings. Pickerel inhabit streams, lakes and ponds, principally in the Northeast. Bass fishermen often catch them in bass waters. Lures and tackle are the same as for bass, but use a short wire leader, or (preferably) a short length of ten-pound-test monofilament. Pickerel have sharp teeth.

Fly-rodders can have fun casting along weed lines with worn bucktails or streamers. Use the old ones you almost threw away; pickerel will strike at almost anything that moves. Flies with Keel hooks or weed guards are needed when casting into holes in grasses and pads.

NORTHERN PIKE

Northern pike are found in most of Canada and in many parts of the northern United States as far west as the Continental Divide. Their average weight is between ten and fifteen pounds. Their ferocity drives other game-fish away from areas in which they live.

Pike are not fussy about water temperatures but prefer water in the 60- to 75-degree range. When weather is near freezing they may be in fairly deep water, but they come into weedy shallows in spring to spawn and remain in such places until winter. In winter they are taken through the ice, usually over weed beds ten to twenty feet deep. In warmer weather they are found in the weedy shallows of bays and coves, usually over weed beds near the shade of logs, pads and grasses. Their favored areas are near their food supply, which consists of smaller fish, also frogs, small animals and floating birds.

Pike are taken on any tackle suitable for large bass. As a guard against their sharp teeth, use a short wire leader, or one of about thirty-pound-test monofilament. I have seen fishermen frustrated in excellent pike areas because they used large spoons which sank too quickly and got caught in weeds. Of course the trick there is to use floating plugs or shallow divers. The most fun is to use surface poppers and to see pike rise and smash at them. In a good pike area you only have to fan-cast from a drifting or anchored boat; any pike that sees the lure will go for it. The speed of retrieve or the action given to the lure make little difference, but alternate from slow to fast until you see what produces best.

Some fishermen think they have taken a muskellunge when they have caught a pike. The muskie has scales on only the upper halves of its cheeks and gill covers. A pike's scales completely cover its cheeks, but only the upper halves of its gill covers. The pickerel's scales cover both cheeks and gill covers. There are other differences, but the three can't be identified by size.

MUSKELLUNGE

The behemoth of the pike family is the muskellunge, which can weigh fifty pounds or more. A fish a yard long and a bit over ten pounds is a small one, hardly considered a "keeper" in many areas. Muskie country is roughly the states around the Great Lakes, including Canada, but the muskie's range is spreading and they may be found as far south as the Tennessee Valley.

Fishermen have been known to fish for muskie for several seasons without ever hooking one. On the other hand, there are specialists who catch them regularly. Anglers without experience who want to try the sport should employ a guide, who will know more than can be provided here.

Unlike pike, which usually run in schools, the muskie is a solitary fish which stakes a claim to several acres of water and drives others of its species away. Possessing a seemingly insatiable appetite, the muskie preys on everything that it can catch. In its private domain the muskie will find a hideaway such as the roots of a dead tree, a log jam or a hole in the weeds and only leave in order to find food. Thus a swirl without a take indicates a muskie's abode, which should be marked and fished again.

Like pike, muskellunge are primarily shallow-water fish. They spawn in the shallows in spring and only go to deeper water temporarily when the shallows rise above 75 degrees in summer. Sixty-five degrees is good muskie water. This is weedy, brushy or stumpy water in the quiet coves of big rivers; structure near the edges of pools below waterfalls, near rocky ledges, and in weedy, lily-padded bays often congested with stumps and logs. In such places trolling may be impractical, so anglers have to hunt their prey by looking for likely spots in the hope of finding the one among many inhabited by a big fish, and inducing it to strike.

When trolling is practical and permitted, several lines are used to pull lures at different depths. Strong plugcasting tackle is preferred for this work.

Casters prospect for muskies somewhat as hunters roam the woods trying to outguess deer. Roaming the shallows in small boats, they cast their lures into possible muskie lairs and hope for an explosive strike. As for trolling, we need heavy plugcasting equipment, with rods having backbone enough to set sharp hooks into bony jaws and to work strong fish away from weeds and roots. Lines should test between twenty and fifty pounds, tipped with a foot or so of metal or monofilament leader testing at least sixty pounds. Muskies have sharp teeth!

Handling hooked northern pike and muskies requires caution. After thrashing around they can be reeled in easily, but don't presume that they have given up. When brought to gaff they begin to thrash again with full vigor, rattling treble-hooked plugs so violently that barbs can impale careless handlers. They also are adept at streaking under the boat and smashing tackle. Keep them out a good distance under strong tension, backing the boat if necessary, until you are sure they are completely played out. Estimate the time at about a minute to the pound.

WALLEYED PIKE

Always delicious to eat and often hard to catch, the sporty walleyed pike isn't a pike at all, but a member of the perch family. Its range, east of the Rockies, covers a large part of central North America. Walleyes average between two and five pounds, but experts often catch bigger ones.

Walleyes are bottom-huggers, preferring rock, gravel or sand, but in some lakes they may lie over mud. Their eyes are poorly adapted to bright light conditions, and therefore they inhabit the shallows only at night or when the water is cloudy, the sky overcast or the surface disturbed by waves. Walleyes do see lures readily, but they also depend on sound and smell to locate food.

In spring after ice leaves the lakes, and when water temperatures are between 45 and 50 degrees, walleyes enter the shallows of lakes or run up tributary streams to spawn. In lakes they seek gravel shorelines, usually near sharply sloping or deep drop-offs, where they lay eggs in shallow water, then leave them alone to hatch. They tolerate water between 55 and 70 degrees, but prefer a temperature of around 60.

Walleyes in rivers are found in the edges of currents (particularly below islands), in sand or gravel channels, in deep holes, along rocky ledges and outcropping, near dead trees in water and in the dropoffs below stream mouths.

Once we camped in Canada in late spring on a lake beside a stream mouth to fish for brook trout. A French gentleman in the party turned up his nose at a big broiled brook trout and would take a fly rod rigged with a streamer fly and small spinner and cast across the stream mouth, allowing the fly to sink and then retrieving it slowly. One cast nearly always provided a walleye of three pounds or better, which he cooked for his dinner. He maintained that walleyes tasted much better than trout, and some of the other anglers agreed with him. At other times in walleye country we have caught all we wanted under the drop-offs of stream mouths. The trick here and everywhere else in walleye fishing is to fish the lure along the bottom. Walleyes are bottom feeders. While spring provides the best streammouth fishing, this depends on water temperatures, which may be compatible in such places all during the season.

Finding walleyes in lakes, regardless of season, is a matter of locating proper temperature depths and suitable structure. The fish may lie shallow in spring and fall in water of about 60 degrees between four and ten feet deep. We know that this is influenced by light conditions. In summer this temperature may be between twenty and forty feet.

Suitable structures in lakes are rocky or gravel bottoms, drop-offs, rocky outcroppings, riprapping, submerged rocky points, bars, ledges and reefs.

Among the best are drop-offs leading to shallows where walleyes can come in to feed at night.

Walleyes travel in schools of fish of similar size. A good way to locate them is to troll slowly over these structures, allowing lures to bounce bottom. One way to troll slowly is to run the boat in reverse. This allows the transom to act as a buffer and also keeps lines clear of the propeller.

Many types of tackle can be used for walleyes, but my choice is a medium-action spinning rod with line testing between six and eight pounds. A good trolling rig is made by attaching a three-way swivel to the end of the line. Attach a bell sinker on about ten inches of lighter monofilament to the lower swivel. Attach a three-foot leader to the upper one, with your choice of lure on it. The sinker should be only heavy enough to bounce bottom.

Small, live baitfish are popular. These are rigged for trolling by using a fine-wire No. 2 hook and impaling the minnow upward through both lips. Walleyes strike bait very lightly, so fishing with minnows is a bit of a trick. We must learn to feel the difference between the light strike and the sinker bouncing on bottom. When in doubt, treat it as a "take" and give line to allow the fish to turn the bait in its mouth and swallow it. Then strike hard.

Another favorite trolling lure, particularly in summer, is a nightcrawler or a few worms on a worm harness. This varies somewhat, but a worm harness is about three hooks in tandem on monofilament with a small spinner at the head, midsection, and rear. This eliminates learning the trick of striking because the hooks solve the problem. Since the fish's sense of smell is important, fresh baits should be used often.

Another good trolling lure is the safety pin recommended for bass. A Rattlelure slip sinker can be put on to add the enticement of sound. The hook rides upward and is either weedless or dressed so it rarely hangs up.

Plugs and spoons are used both for trolling and casting. Popular ones include the Rapala, Flatfish, River Runt, Bomber and Thinfin. The famous Dardevle is used occasionally, but spinners and spoons are not the most effective lures for walleyes. Many fishermen add worms or other baits to the tail hooks of plugs, if this doesn't interfere with the action. Retrieves should be steady and as slow as proper action permits.

When walleyes are located by trolling, anglers anchor their boat and cast for the fish. Bait should be fished at proper depth with bobbers. The bait should hang as close to bottom as possible. Minnows, hooked just below the dorsal fin, are effective. Put a split shot on the line a foot or so above the bait to keep it down. Other good baits are worms, nightcrawlers, leeches, hellgrammites, crayfish and even small frogs.

Jigs are considered the most effective lures for walleyes. The hook may be sweetened with bait, but three inches of plastic worm, partly strung on the shank to expose bend and barb, is currently in great favor.

9

The Senses of Fish

Finding fish is of course only part of the angling game; enticing them to strike a natural bait or artificial lure is almost all of the rest. And it is here that a knowledge of the fish's sensory equipment is helpful—how it responds to scent, sound and sight. For many an angler returns empty-handed simply because he frightened a fish that would have struck or because he chose the wrong lure for the situation.

The senses of mammals, birds and insects are far more finely tuned and developed than are those of humans, so let's not underestimate the senses of fish. In their fascinating book on fish behavior, *Through the Fish's Eye* (by this publisher), co-authors Mark Sosin and John Clark state that two-hundredths of a drop of extract from a seal's skin can be detected by salmon in a 23,000-gallon swimming pool—or in a pool of the same size in a river. We know that tagged salmon smolts can travel thousands of miles in the ocean and return after years at sea to the same river and its tributary in which they were born. Those who underestimate the senses of fish, or fail to comprehend them, pay the penalty of failing to catch them.

THE SENSE OF SIGHT

In some older angling books we read that fish are color-blind, seeing lures only in shades of gray. This isn't so, according to modern science, which finds the retinal structure of fish similar to that of humans.

For example, an experiment was conducted with panels of different colors in an aquarium of goldfish. The fish were taught in a matter of hours that they would be fed if they nosed the red panel, but that no food would result from nosing the others. Panels were shifted and colors were varied from intense to pale, yet the fish always nosed the red or pink one to obtain food. We now know that fish have acute sight and accurate color perception, although it varies slightly among the various species.

Knowledgeable anglers wear dull-colored clothing, avoiding bright colors and white in favor of tan, green and gray. Knowledgeable anglers keep their silhouettes low because light refraction in water enable fish to see them. Unbelievers can walk slowly and quietly to streamside and watch fish scoot for cover. Thus, wading anglers have an advantage over bank fishermen: the deeper they wade, the lower their silhouette.

In doing research for this book, I tried to find authentic information about color selection of lures under various conditions. I talked or corresponded with many famous anglers, and read numerous books on fish behavior and angling. Many of the answers I got were contradictory, but I was able to find sufficient agreement to formulate a few theories of my own.

In surface or near-surface fishing we imitate whatever fish are (or should be) feeding on. Thus we know that dry flies, wet flies and nymphs imitate the naturals in shape and color. We select streamers and bucktails that imitate the colors, shapes and sizes of prevalent baitfish. Minnowlike and froglike plugs are selected the same way. However, questions pop up in other areas. When selecting an attractor pattern in streamer flies, should we choose yellow and red, white and blue, or something else? When selecting a plug, should we choose an all-black one or a red and white one, or should we try yellow or another of the dozens of color schemes provided by manufacturers? These decisions depend on the brightness of the day, the depth and clarity of the water, and other factors.

Let's recall the colors of the spectrum, as seen in a rainbow. The red end of the spectrum has a long wavelength and low reflectance; that is, the colors at this end disappear more quickly the deeper they are fished. This is because water is a poor conductor of light. In clear water light doesn't penetrate much beyond thirty feet or so, and in cloudy water barely ten feet. Thus red and orange are visible near the surface but not in deep water. On the other hand, the colors at the blue end of the spectrum have short wavelengths and high reflectance, so these can be seen more clearly in deep water.

Now let's look at the non-colors from black to white. Black, like red, has a long wavelength and low reflectance, while white is just the opposite. Shades of gray, like those of yellow, are in the middle range.

What does this prove? To me it doesn't prove very much about using black-red (low-reflectance colors) near the surface because there fish are influenced by sunlight and the clearness of the water. The main point is that short-wavelength, high-reflectance colors (the blues and greens) can be seen better by fish in deep water.

Some experts don't agree with this in spite of scientific evidence. They think black lures are effective in deep water. Others agree, and use blue and white lures for deep fishing. Chartreuse, which is light green (green and white) with a little yellow, is currently the favorite in plastic worms. Before chartreuse became fashionable, blue and purple, which are about the same, were popular. For deep saltwater jigging many experts prefer white or green. Thus the short-wave colors seem more popular than the long-wave ones for deep water.

On bright days in clear water the best non-imitative fly is a light one with plenty of tinsel. This is because in sunlight the sides of baitfish are reflective and shimmer and shine as they twist and turn while gathering food. Lures should be silver, or another light color. However, this can be carried too far. A highly polished silver or nickel spoon, for example, can have too much flash in bright sunlight, and can send fish to cover.

On bright days in discolored water (or dull ones in clear water) fly and lure selection is in the middle range. Flies should be dull (gray) with less tinsel, usually only as a ribbing. Spoons and spinners should be less flashy, and plugs in middle-range colors. My practice is to let metal lures tarnish and to rub them to proper flash with crocus cloth when need be. Tarnished ones rubbed to moderate flash are excellent under these conditions.

Another favorite practice of mine in the above situations is to use flies with a bit of fluorescence on them, usually as a butt. Other lures can have fluorescent beads. Fluorescence is emanated according to light reflection. Use none or only a bit under bright conditions. On dull days or in discolored water we can afford more.

On dull days in discolored water flies should be dark with no tinsel, lures dark with no flash, or else just a bit.

All this depends on the actinic value of light and its direction and influence on the water. When two or more persons are fishing together one can fish by the rules; others can experiment until they find the right lure.

Another widespread opinion is that dull flies are more effective in warm water (over 50 degrees) and that brighter ones are better in colder water (under 50 degrees). This may apply to other lures.

Nearly everyone agrees we should use large flies and lures in heavy water, medium sized ones in normal flow, and small ones in low water. This is merely a matter of using lures that fish can see easily.

Anglers who fish for brown trout and other species at night prefer lures that are black through gray to white. They prefer black or dark lures on dark nights, grayish lures during half-moon periods, and white lures when the moon is about full. At night I would opt for dark lures all the time. During World War II, frogmen told me that the ships' hulls which were hardest to see from below were the white ones. This is the reason for white (or very light) fly lines. Black or dark lines on the water are easily seen from below. We know that black is the "color" that reflects the least light, that white reflects the most. From this, readers can draw their own conclusions.

Finally, as far as color selection goes, the popular Dardevle wobbler sells best in red and white, although it comes in many other color combinations. Red and white also are popular colors for other lures, such as plugs and flies. Why? The two colors are entirely opposite in reflectance value so one is seen more clearly when the other is not, making the combination of more or less universal value.

THE SENSE OF HEARING

Although their acoustical organs are concealed, fish can hear sounds more acutely and over a wider range than humans can. (Also, sound travels five times faster in water than it does in air.) Scientists say that fish can hear nymphs crawling on rocks, and will swim to the source of the sound to feed.

Anglers who noisily approach a stream usually find it "fishless." I recall a time after lunch on a wilderness stream in Maine when I was sitting on a small bluff, watching trout and baitfish in a pool. A big trout lying between the edges of a rock would rise periodically to pick insects from the surface. Several other trout were peacefully resting or feeding here and there, but I waited for cloudier conditions before starting the afternoon's fishing. Suddenly the big trout disappeared under a ledge of the rock, and all the others scooted for safety. Minnows stopped feeding, and their actions became erratic. I had heard nothing but the peaceful sounds around me.

Then a branch snapped upstream and a rock bounced noisily into the river. An angler pushed his way through the undergrowth; dropped clumsily into the stream, and started casting. He fished lies where trout had been, but hooked nothing. Finally seeing me, he came over for a visit.

"Lousy fishing," he remarked, lighting a cigar. "You catch anything?"

"Not lately," I replied, hoping he wouldn't notice the long spine and ribs of the only one I hadn't put back. The bones had nearly burned in the embers of a small fire on the pebble beach.

After a bit of conversation the fisherman stood up and stretched.

"Guess I'll mosey down to the pool below, if you don't want to fish it right now."

He nodded and was gone.

I quenched the dying embers of the fire and scuffed gravel to conceal it completely. Then I took a short nap. As I awoke a cloud bank from the west obscured the sun. The big trout had resumed feeding and some smaller ones had reappeared. I slowly wriggled down the bluff to the protection of alder bushes and dropped a dry fly upstream of the rock where the big one lay. The fly fluttered down, drifted close to the rock, and the fish rose and took it. I backed the barb from his jaw and watched him swim away.

The story is related to remind us that a noisy approach usually results in poor fishing, or none at all. Anglers who wade quietly rarely alarm fish; rocks disturbed on the stream beds are natural sounds. Anglers who clump along the bank make unnatural sounds which put fish down. Water is an excellent conductor of sound, and we know that sound travels fast underwater.

Boat fishermen have a similar problem, although few realize it. The best way *not* to catch fish is to cut the motor over the hole; throw out the anchor; bang open the tackleboxes, drop a beer can on the deck . . . you get the point.

Another mistake is to cast your lure too close to a fish. The plop of a plug, or even a wobbler or a spinner, can frighten it. Cast beyond the suspected hide and fish the lure into position. Of course there are exceptions to this. The quiet *splat* of a lure landing on the surface can attract fish. Frogs and even baitfish often make similar sounds. This is especially true at night, or in discolored water, because under these conditions fish feed mainly by sound and scent.

Lures That Make Noise

Since fish feed by sound as well as by sight, lures are available that pop, splutter, chug, buzz, rattle, splash and vibrate. Even plastic worms give off sound audible to fish when inched and bounced along the bottom. Let's review some typical ones:

Sonic lures are fish-shaped plugs with one or more attachment eyes on the top of the body slightly forward of the dorsal fin position. By attaching the line to forward, middle or rear eyes, the lure can be fished at different

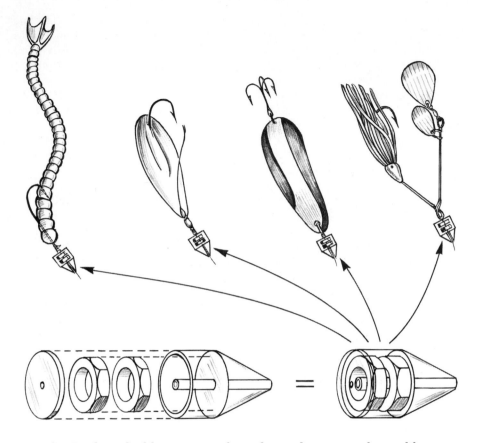

The Rattlure doubles as a weight and sound attractor, the nutlike insert rattling inside the plastic cone as the lure is fished. It can be added to a plastic worm, spoon, or safety-pin lure. *Courtesy Burke Fishing Lures.*

depths with varying vibrations. These lures may have a vibrator sound chamber to make them rattle or vibrate as the lure swims, but some emit only pulsating vibrations.

Spinners emit vibrations or pulsations to some degree. With their flashing, whirling blades, we think of them more as visual attractors, but heavily-bladed ones, such as the famous Mepps, also give off strong sound vibrations.

An instance of how sound attracts fish occurred on a canal off the Tamiami Trail on Florida's southern coast. The water was as discolored as it can get, a coffee-and-cream shade in which lures couldn't be seen inches under the surface. This was brackish water holding snook. We were using streamer flies and not catching anything. I switched to a large brass spinner and took fish on almost every cast. When the others switched to pulsating lures they did the same. The place was loaded, but no fish were taken on lures that didn't emit sound. My final one was an 18-pound, 14-ounce whopper that happened to top its class in the Metropolitan Miami Fishing Tournament that year. The point is that it was impossible for fish to see lures and that they took them only by sound. Don't underestimate the value of sound in discolored water.

Spinners on plugs splutter and splash on the surface, vibrate underneath, attracting fish by their sound. Underwater plugs that wiggle also give off sound vibrations. So do swimming baitfish.

Splashers are surface plugs which should be in every tacklebox. The Jitterbug is a famous example. Its wide double lip pushes water, while causing the plug to swim with a seductive wiggle.

Poppers are available from tiny fly-rod size to large ones used in salt water. When activated, they push the surface with a popping sound which adds to the visual effect.

Rattling lures are of relatively recent origin, and very effective regardless of water clarity. They are particularly useful in cloudy water and/or when fished deep. An excellent example is the Rattlure, which doubles as a weight and a sound producer. My favorite use for it is to weight a plastic worm. It also helps when spinners or wobblers must be fished deep.

In summarizing the hearing sense of fish, three points stand out. The hearing of fish is amazingly acute. Anglers who make too much noise can ruin their fishing. Lures that produce sound are particularly effective in deep or discolored water.

Sound-Producing Lures

Popping plug with a concave head

Sonic plug with vibrating sound chamber

Spluttering plug with double-lobed lip

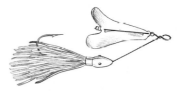

Safety-pin lure, pulsates on retrieve

THE SENSE OF SMELL

Science affirms that the sense of smell in fish is highly developed, more so in some species than in others. An example was given of the acute sense of smell of salmon, which can find their rivers by following the faint, familiar scent they remember after years at sea. The food morsels thrown into the water in chumming attract fish more by their scent than by the sight of the food itself. Sharks can zero in on faint smells of blood in the water and find the source from far away.

Fish can detect and identify unseen members of their own species by their peculiar scent. Fish can also detect and find prey by scent. Some fish have repulsive odors, given them by heredity as a means of protection. We can rarely smell schools of fish in streams and lakes, either because we can't identify the odor or because the schools are too small to make it apparent. Expert saltwater anglers, however, often find big schools of fish by scent. A school of striped bass gives off an unmistakable odor of the herb called thyme. A school of bluefish can be found by the distinctive odor of cut melons wafting downwind.

In early spring, when streams are high and cold, experienced bait fishermen catch more trout than do anglers who use artificial lures. The trout are resting in holding positions, and the bait must be presented to them so they can *smell* it even if they don't at first see it. To do this, cast upstream of the rock so the bait will sink and drift between the edges back of the rock. Casting *to* the rock won't work; the bait drifts above the fish and touches bottom, if at all, all too far downstream. The bait must be fresh to have maximum scent. A worm used a long time may look satisfactory, and may take fish by sight, but chances are much better with a fresh one which provides scent. If you are short of worms, puncture an old one with a hook so more scent can exude from it.

Scent has a bearing on taste. If a lure looks good a fish may take it, but will quickly expel it if it has an obnoxious taste. I have noticed on many occasion that trout and salmon will go for a fly but won't take it. We all know that fish may nip at flies without being hooked. It seems logical that this is because of taste, and fish dislike the taste emanated by humans.

We can all remember times when we are sure that we have selected the correct fly or lure and are doing everything else right, but we get no strikes until we have been fishing for a considerable time. While there may be other reasons for this, one could be that the fly or lure isn't taken until its obnoxious scent has been washed off.

Old-time commercial fishermen learned that it helps to dip lures in cod liver oil. One chap who I'm sure is a good friend sent me a small bottle of seal oil, supposedly to dip salmon flies in. A mere drop of this stuff in a salmon river will alarm fish far downstream because seals are enemies of salmon. At the same time he sent me a small bottle of salmon oil, which may be useful. I'll take both bottles when I go fishing with him and ask him to dip his flies in them after I've hooked my limit!

Plastic worms are scented, usually with an extract of anise, which tastes like licorice. This is known to be an attractive scent to fish, although no one knows exactly why.

Fish in general, and particularly trout and salmon, find human scent repellent. For this reason, some anglers wash their hands on land before going astream. Sosin and Clark state that while human scent is repulsive to fish, human saliva isn't, and that artificial flies will be taken more readily if they are moistened on the tongue. This evidently substantiates the old maxim that "You'll have better luck if you spit on your bait!"

10

How to Rig and Use Natural Baits

Fly fishermen and bait addicts don't always agree, the former scorning the use of bait as unsportsmanlike, the latter maintaining that the point is to catch fish and have fun.

When streams are cold, high and discolored, the fisherman who can drift a worm (or other bait) along the bottom into a good holding position usually scores while those who use flies, plugs or metal lures don't do too well. Later in the season, when conditions are right, artificials do best, one of the reasons being that the lure is in the water more often.

While everyone is entitled to his opinion, it doesn't pay to be dogmatic. Try all methods and find the ones most satisfying. In the seventeenth century, Izaak Walton, a bait fisherman, befriended Charles Cotton, who preferred artificial flies. Each respected the other's opinions and both remain famous today.

Some natural baits do better under certain conditions or for specific species of fish than do others. Some baits are available when others are not. There are different ways to rig and fish each kind of bait.

TACKLE FOR BAIT FISHING

While experienced bait fishermen may become wedded to one method or another, there are some guidelines for increasing strikes.

For fishing streams, consider the advantages of the fly rod. A short, light rod can be poked through foliage along small streams where a short drift of the bait into good holding positions may be all that is necessary or possible. When lack of obstructions permits flipping baits longer distances, a longer and stronger fly rod is preferable; in wide streams, the longer the better. With added length we can guide the bait down feed lanes on either side of us, reaching out to work it around rocks, guiding it into obstructions such as fallen trees, or probing the hot spots below undercut banks. The advantages of the long rod, as compared to shorter spinfishing or spinning gear, is illustrated by the fact that some experts in America, and many in Europe, use rods (or poles) as long as twelve feet or more to guide baits more accurately. More about the tackle and tactics for this kind of fishing will be discussed later.

While the fly rod has decided advantages in small to medium-sized streams, it is much less valuable in really wide ones. Here we need spinning or spincasting gear for the longer casts necessary to sweep baits down wide stretches and to fish them near the bottom of deep pools and runs where prize fish so often lie. The finer diameter monofilament lines also drag less and drift baits more naturally after long casts. The choice between spinning, spincasting or baitcasting gear is more or less a personal one. Spinning gear, however, does have an advantage over the other methods when light lines and lures are used.

At first glance, using the fly rod for bait fishing seems only as simple as putting a worm on a hook and drifting it into a likely lie. Those who habitually hook trophy trout know there is more to it than that. Let's see how they do it. There are three methods, all of which are effective depending on fishing conditions.

The Fly Rod with a Floating Line

This method is similar to, but more precise than, the usual way of using fly rods for bait fishing which anglers have been employing for many generations. Knowledgeable water readers will find that it brings more strikes from bigger fish. It is particularly adaptable for fast streams and provides excellent results in the high water run-offs of the early season.

All we need is a long fly rod (8–9½ feet) with a standard reel and a double-tapered floating line. Attach a level leader (regular monofilament of about four-pound test) to the line with a Nail Knot or a Leader Whip Knot. The leader should be at least as long as the rod. The knot must be smooth enough to pass through the guides easily, and it helps to coat it with fluorescent paint for noting strikes.

Tie a small, short-shanked hook to the leader's end, remembering that it should be unobtrusive and buried in the bait as far as possible consistent with hooking ability. Add a bit of lead about a foot and a half above the hook, and perhaps another bit or two spaced farther up on the leader. The kind and amount of lead is important.

My favorite lead is the twist-on strips about the shape of paper book matches, readily available in folders like common match books. Tear off a strip, cut it in two, and wrap half a strip on the leader, perhaps using the other half farther up. Wound around the leader neatly, with ends crimped with the thumbnail, the strips rarely catch on anything. Other leads, such as split shot, can be used, but I don't consider them as good.

The right amount of lead is of primary importance to work bait near bottom without its catching too frequently. Use enough small bits of spaced lead to get the bait down, but remove a little if it catches. If catch-ups are chronic anyway (as happens on very rocky streams) the alternative is to tie in a short dropper and to add to its end a pinch-on lead or two which can be pulled off if they become snagged. This is similar to what steelhead anglers do when they use a pencil lead on a dropper lighter than the line.

This rig can be cast upstream, downstream or cross-stream. When cast

Downstream worming with a fly rod. To work his bait deep, the fisherman checks his forward cast and gives line so it forms several S-curves. While these are straightening out, he pulls more slack line from the reel and allows the bait to drift at current speed.

upstream, the line must be retrieved fast enough to keep it tight. You can follow the progress of the bait by watching the floating line. When the line hesitates during a drift, strike quickly. Of course the bait must be drifted at current speed regardless of the direction it is fished. Use only enough lead to fish the bait on or near bottom, and maintain line control so you can feel a strike.

When fishing with this rig, we sometimes find that the bait sinks and won't drift naturally in slow runs or pools. A natural drift can be achieved here by using a small, light sponge-rubber bobber. This type is less of an impediment to casting than most, but still it should be used only when necessary. The bobber should be only large enough to hold up the bait so when a fish takes the lure it feels little or no resistance. If, when a fish strikes, the bobber jerks back, the fish knows the bait is unnatural and usually refuses it.

While a floating line is superior for most stream fishing, a floating one with a sinking tip may be advisable for deep water. Avoid sinking lines, however; they make it difficult to feel and handle strikes.

The Fly Rod with Monofilament
Monofilament lines have added a new dimension to bait fishing with fly rods. Readers may not like it as well as the previous method, but they may

A light bobber rig for bait fishing with a fly rod. The bobber is made
of sponge rubber and is so light that it barely interferes with casting.
Sinker between bobber and bait is optional.

find it offers certain advantages. The long fly rod can be used with a fly
reel, spinning reel, or spincasting reel.

When using the fly reel, attach to the line a spool of monofilament of
three- or four-pound test; the lighter, the better. Wind on thirty feet or
more. The length isn't important, but it should be more than can be cast.
Before fishing, stretch the monofilament to avoid coils. Add hook and bait
as previously, but avoid adding lead unless necessary, and then only the
minimum amount. Bobbers can also be used as previously described, and
for the same reasons.

This rig can be used in upstream, cross-stream or downstream fishing,
but its main advantage is in providing a natural downstream drift. Casts
are made with as much line out as the length of the rod. More can't be
cast conveniently, but a considerable amount can be pulled from the reel,
controlled by thumb and forefinger of the line hand, and shot out during
the cast, or payed out during the downstream drift.

"Cast" probably isn't the correct word here, because the bait is
"lobbed," rather than cast. Hold the monofilament to prevent much more
than a rod's length going out. Then flip the bait back, letting it touch the
water, and lob it forward, releasing the slack.

For drifting baits downstream, many think that monofilament handles
easier than a fly line and leader. By extending, raising or lowering the rod
the bait can be guided into pockets and runs and other holding positions.
The method is excellent for probing dark areas below undercut banks where
big fish so often lie. Downstream drifts can cover a lot of area, straight
down, and to the right or left.

In upstream fishing the bait can be lobbed at least two rod lengths,
and practice can improve this. As the line is stripped in it is controlled by
pressing it against the rod grip with the forefinger. In cross-stream fishing
the principles are the same. The advantage is that the fine diameter mono-

Cross-stream worming with a fly rod. This deep canyon pool has strongly defined current edges, submerged rocks, and eddies against the rocky cliff. It would be difficult to fish this pool from below or above; a cross-stream cast from a crouched position on the opposite bank is the best bet. The trick is to drift the bait along each edge, A and B, and allow the current to sweep it downstream without drag.

filament doesn't drag in the current like a fly line and whip the lure.

Spinning or spincasting reels can also be used with the fly rod; they are more convenient for fishing downstream. Since the reel is on the grip behind the hand, this may seem awkward at first, but awkwardness disappears with experience. In downstream fishing either type of reel can release line as freely as the current takes the bait to provide a natural drift. Line can be controlled by the forefinger of the rod hand, and can be snubbed by it when the angler wants to strike or to hold the lure in position. The line can be put under control of the reel instantly, whereupon the fish is handled as usual with the type of reel being used. This method combines the line control afforded by a spinning reel with the pleasure of playing a fish on a fly rod.

Longer rods, then, aid us in guiding baits where we want them to go. The idea is ancient, but often ignored by modern fishermen. Old books illustrate rods sixteen feet or even longer, used for precise placement and drifting of baits. While this was the main reason for them, lack of adequate reels was another. We know that the idea continues in cane-pole fishing, but we may not realize that light fiberglass poles about twelve feet long, equipped with tiny spool-like reels holding only a small quantity of mono-filament, are not uncommon on some trout streams today. Users extend only about five or six feet of line from the rod tip, drop the slightly weighted bait into a run, and fish it down by swinging the long pole at current speed to get perfect drifts with the bait bouncing bottom. These anglers often can exhibit creels of big fish that are the envy and astonishment of anglers using other methods. Purists will frown at this; I only report it. Izaak Walton used the same technique in the seventeenth century, and others did before him. In some respects angling hasn't changed very much!

SPINNING AND SPINCASTING HINTS

Although spinning and spincasting tackle and techniques are discussed extensively in my previous book *Fishing* and elsewhere, some confusion still exists between the two methods, which are quite different from each other.

The spinning reel has an open face and a fixed spool from which the line spirals off unimpeded until slowed down or stopped by forefinger pressure and closing the bail. Rods have large ring guides to aid smooth outflow of line and they are moderately stiff for accurate, long-distance casting. This relative lack of friction, or drag, allows longer casts with lighter lines and lures.

The spincasting reel, on the other hand, has a closed face from which the line peels off to pass through a small hole in the center of the spool's cover, or hood. This adds considerable friction but eliminates excess line spiraling off prematurely to cause snarls, a problem in spinning which can be avoided. Rods are shorter than those used in spinning, similar to plug-casting rods. Thus, to get much distance in spincasting, we must use heavier lures and relatively stronger lines.

The spincasting method is considered more foolproof for novices, but the longer casts with lighter lines and lures (or baits) strongly recommends spinning. There's more to it than that. Fishermen who habitually use lures which should be retrieved erratically, and who often fish in dense cover, should find spincasting gear more acceptable. Those who use lures which can be retrieved more or less smoothly, and who rarely fish in dense cover, should choose spinning tackle. Success with spinning tackle requires that the line be retrieved under fairly constant tension to pack it smoothly on the reel spool. It is difficult to do this when using surface popping plugs or other lures that are bucktailed on the retrieve.

Worm Fishing with Fixed-Spool Tackle

With spinning and spincasting tackle, somewhat heavier terminal tackle—baits, leads and floats—is needed. These help us to fish deeper, at the right temperature levels.

The most successful worm fishermen don't dig and use their bait the same day. They let them lie in moss, damp leaves or commercial worm bedding long enough to scour themselves of ingested dirt and body slime. This leaves them a bright pink or red and tougher and livelier on the hook.

Fishing bait with spinning tackle. The angler has reached the bank at lower right and notices a shaded undercut bank on the left shore — ideal cover for trout. The technique here is to cast close to the shoreline, to point A, and leave the reel in free spool so line can be released and the bait can drift freely downstream. Keep the line from overspilling by light forefinger pressure on the spool. On a strike, exert firm pressure, raise the rod tip, and close the bail.

Remember to use small, short-shank hooks which can be concealed in the bait as much as possible, hooking worms only once, through the collar.

Drift the worm naturally with the current into holding positions, leaving the pickup open so line can peel off the reel. The outflow is controlled by forefinger pressure on spinning reels and by finger and thumb pressure on spincasting reels. On a strike the line can quickly be put under control of the reel. There is a bit of an art to releasing line properly and still feeling strikes, but this is easily learned. When enough line has been released, put it under control of the reel and let the lure hang downstream momentarily. A fish following it might then pick it up. Retrieve it slowly, through edges and holding positions where possible. Although it isn't natural for worms to travel upstream, their appearance and smell may make hungry fish forget this.

Fishing a worm upstream can be more productive than fishing downstream or quartering downstream. By casting upstream or quartering upstream the bait drifts down naturally and bumps bottom in fast currents. The trick is to retrieve all slack line without pulling the bait, except when necessary to guide it above a target so it will drift down into it. If the bait lodges on bottom in slower currents, a tighter line may be needed to keep it off gravel or rocks.

Bobbers are helpful for fishing worms in deep pools and runs; also in ponds and lakes. When a bobber is set far up on the line it is difficult to cast. The illustration shows how a small button can be used as a bobber stop. String the button on the monofilament; string on the sliding bobber, and add a split shot or two a foot or so above the bait. In casting, the bobber is against the split shot, so it doubles as a casting weight. In the water, the bait and shot sink and the bobber rises up the line to be stopped at the button. The button can be slid along the monofilament to regulate depth. Of course this rig can be used with minnows and other baits.

A bobber is used to suspend bait at a desired depth. It is not needed in currents fast enough to carry bait, but is helpful in drifting bait down a languid pool, or to suspend it over a weedy bottom where it will drift in the breeze.

How to Fish Nightcrawlers

Readers who use nightcrawlers may have noticed that, after a cast or two, the bait is doubled unnaturally on the hook. Fish rarely take it in this condition. The bait must look natural and must drift naturally for best

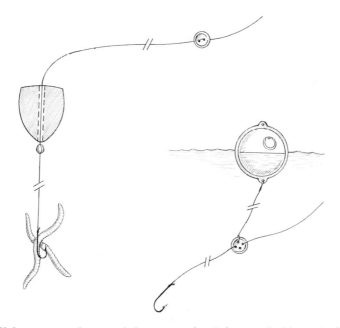

Small button used as a sliding stop for fishing a bobber. At left, float is strung on line above split shot for easier casting, but slides up line to button when in the water. At right, a water-weighted bubble float attached to button with a short piece of monofilament. Depth of bait can be regulated by sliding button on the line.

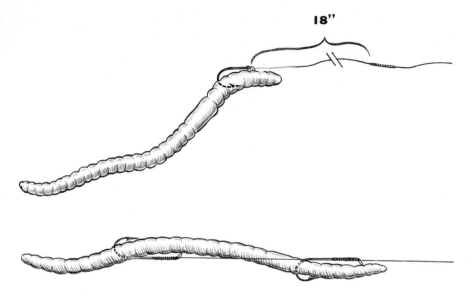

Two rigs for fishing nightcrawlers. Top, small short-shanked hook buried in head of worm allows it to act more naturally in the water. Below is a tandem rig to foil bait stealers.

results. Use bright, well scoured crawlers and replace them when they become inactive. Use small, short-shanked hooks, concealed in the bait as much as possible. When water conditions permit, let the bait drift and sink naturally, without lead, or keep weight to a minimum.

Two effective rigs for nightcrawlers are illustrated. In the first, the small, short-shanked hook is buried in the head of the worm, rather than through the collar. This allows the bait to act more naturally, but it also encourages bait stealers. If lead is necessary, I prefer the Twist-On type (discussed earlier) about eighteen inches above the bait.

When small, bait-stealing fish are not present this is the best rig. Fish it on a taut line so you can feel taps. When a fish starts to take the bait, give it line and delay the strike until you guess the bait has been ingested. Then strike hard; the crawler may be wrapped around the hook and the barb must penetrate it to set in the fish's jaw.

When small bait-stealing fish make this single-hook rig impractical, use the tandem rig shown in the second drawing. When lead must be used with it a good arrangement is to tie a very small swivel into the line about eighteen inches above the hook, with a sliding sinker above it. The swivel prevents the sinker from sliding down to the bait. The two hooks allow you to strike quicker. Use short-shanked hooks, about size 8.

SALMON EGGS

The best eggs are taken from freshly killed Pacific salmon or steelhead trout when they are ready to spawn. In salmon or steelhead rivers some spawned but uncovered eggs drift downstream and are eagerly sought by fish of all species. In other rivers where spawning does not occur, salmon eggs are still a good trout bait.

When fresh eggs are not available preserved ones are acceptable and are readily found in tackle stores everywhere. Hook the large single ones as shown in the illustration. Since the use of eggs as bait is prohibited in some states, fish and game laws should be consulted.

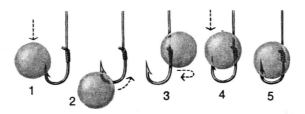

How to hook a salmon egg. Use a short-shanked, fine-wire hook matching the egg size. Bury all but a small part of the bend in the egg by following the steps shown above. *Uncle Josh Bait Co.*

FISHING WITH MINNOWS

Minnows can be fished properly with any light tackle. Most fishermen use spinning or spincasting gear, but old-timers still prefer a fly rod for stream fishing, and for good reason. As with worm fishing, the longer rod can guide the bait into good holding positions with a minimum of line drag.

There are many ways to rig minnows. Live ones can be hooked upward through both lips or under the forward part of the dorsal fin *above* the backbone.

Some methods of sewing on minnows require so many hitches and punctures that the natural appearance of the bait is nearly ruined. The illustration on page 162 shows an effective rig. Push the hook down through the lower lip and draw it out with several inches of monofilament. Push the hook down through the top of the head and draw it out. Push the hook into the middle of the body and make it curve out near the tail, so the entire shank is buried. Holding the bait cupped in the hand, draw all connections tight so the bait maintains a slight curve. It should spin or revolve only very slowly. Too much curve makes it revolve too fast.

Of course we use minnows that have expired, and even preserved ones will do. The bait stays on the hook until a fish mashes it. Let the bait roll and drift into good holding positions, but give it slight action with the rod tip in imitation of a baitfish in distress. This rig is also excellent for trolling.

Another efficient rig can be made with a double hook (page 163). The only tool needed is a long needle. Lacking one, bend a tiny loop in one end of a few inches of stiff stainless-steel wire. Thread several inches of mono-

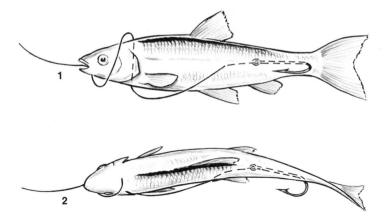

Author's method of sewing on a minnow. (1) Push hook down through lower lip and draw out. Push hook through top to bottom of head and draw out. Push hook into body as far back as possible and push point through body. (2) Carefully tighten monofilament to give minnow a slight curve, which will make it spin. Attach end of monofilament to swivel to prevent line twist.

filament line or leader through the loop (or needle's eye) and push the point into the minnow's mouth through the body and out the vent. With the bait strung on the monofilament, tie a double hook to its end. Push the shank into the bait's vent and body until it is buried there, and tighten the monofilament. The hook's upwardly curved barbs straddle the bait. Hooks should be large enough to make them grab efficiently. Downward pointing ones are preferable in waters where they won't hang up.

When streams are cold, the baits which have been discussed must bounce bottom where the fish usually are. One way to do this is to use enough lead on the line above the bait to take it down in the current. This usually requires an upstream cast, or one quartering upstream. The trick is to keep slack out of the line then, so we can feel the bait bouncing bottom, keep it moving, and also feel strikes.

Another method is borrowed from steelhead fishermen. Tie a small three-way swivel to the line's end. Attach the bait to a foot or more of leader and tie this to one of the swivel's rings. Attach a dipsey sinker or a pencil lead to about half the above amount of leader and fasten this to the third swivel ring. The monofilament which attaches the lead should be considerably weaker than the line so it will break when badly snagged. The strength of the monofilament to which the bait is attached should be between the other two. Hang-ups sometimes are frequent, but all we usually lose is the lead. If the bait snags and can't be pulled loose, it is usually broken at the swivel or at the hook. Remember the old maxim that you aren't fishing deep enough if the bait doesn't snag occasionally, so carry plenty of leads, leaders

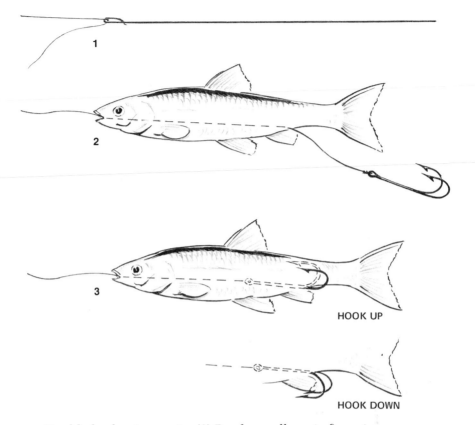

HOOK UP

HOOK DOWN

Double-hook minnow rig. (1) Bend a small eye in fine wire, or use a long needle, and thread on monofilament. (2) Push wire through minnow's mouth and body, out vent, Attach double hook. (3) Pull monofilament out minnow's mouth; push hook shank into body so minnow is between the hooks. Hook points can also face down.

and hooks. Pencil leads snag the least. Keep the line tight so the bouncing lead can be felt as your twitching rod tip guides it down the drift.

We have noted that this rig is often used in trolling when fish are lying on bottom.

Another simple way to hook a minnow for casting is shown in the drawing on page 164. We need a few short-shanked bait hooks, in sizes 1 or 1/0 and preferably offset or double offset. Attach a hook to about a foot of monofilament and attach the monofilament to the line with a small barrel swivel. Run the hook's point into the mouth and out one of the gills. Then turn the hook and push it completely through the body back of the head. Let point and barb emerge.

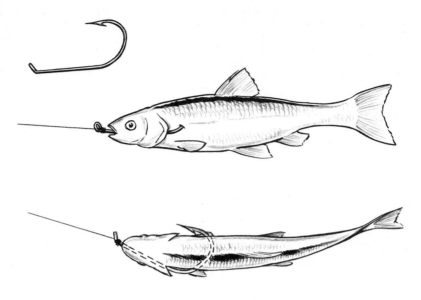

Minnow rig for casting. Use short-shanked bait hook, size 1 or 1/0. Run point into mouth and out gill, then turn hook and push it through body and allow point and barb to emerge. For best results, use a small barrel swivel on monofilament.

This bait should be given slight rod-tip action unless the current is strong. Fish it upstream, or up and across, keeping slack line reeled in so strikes can be felt. If the strike is light, allow momentary slack before setting the hook to allow the fish to take the bait solidly. The first method is preferable for trolling because the rig has built-in action. All can be used for trolling or casting, but the second and third methods work best when action is imparted to the lure.

CRAYFISH: SOMETIMES THE BEST BAIT

Part of the fun of fishing is to visit new places and to learn the methods other anglers use. In some spots the usually popular worms and minnows are spurned because the name of the game there is "crayfish." Call them what you will—crawfish, crawdads or lobsters, among other names—the crayfish during its season is considered by many to be the best bait of all. Small ones take smallmouths; bigger ones tempt largemouths. Trout, walleyes, catfish and perch will grab any crayfish they can get their jaws around.

We don't find crayfish in all waters because some lack proper alkalinity for them to grow and shed their shells properly. Evidently most fish and game departments don't object to our catching crayfish in one place and using them as bait in another, so look around a bit and see if any are in residence. They can be caught in traps (like lobster traps) baited with fish or fish-based cat food. Use a quarter-inch nylon seine to gather them in brooks. Let it bag downstream and scuff rocks above to dislodge the crayfish and drive them into the net.

Use short-shanked hooks in about size 6 for small crayfish, and up to size 2 for bigger ones. One way to hook them is upward through the tail; another, which may keep them alive longer, is to push the hook's point from the rear forward under some of the tail segments. It is important that the bait be fresh, so replace it after every few casts. Fish will ignore dead or nearly dead crayfish.

Crayfish can be kept alive in cool water that is changed frequently. Since they fight each other, and can nip rather painfully, the larger ones should be declawed. To do this, grasp the pincher with fishing pliers; the crayfish will shake off its claw. (It will grow another if it lives.)

How do you fish crayfish? Suppose you are fishing in summer for bass in a lake where they inhabit structure just below the thermocline, which we'll say is at about thirty feet. Use spinning or spincasting tackle with about six-pound-test line, no sinker. Hook the crayfish as explained above, and cast about thirty feet. The bait will try to swim down, going in a quarter circle from the surface to below the boat. Keep the reel's pickup open to give line. You'll feel taps when a fish takes, but let it run because it will pause to swallow the bait tailfirst. That's the time to strike—hard!

Crayfish can be used for smallmouths, trout and walleyes. They try to crawl under rocks, so keep them off bottom where fish can smell and see them.

HELLGRAMMITES

The popular hellgrammite is a mean-looking dark-brown or black water inhabitant which is the larval form of the dobsonfly, sometimes misnamed dragonfly. It has six pairs of legs plus various little claws and feelers and a pair of nippers at front which can bite. It reaches a length of about three inches and can be found under rocks in and near streams.

Frequently during a lull in noonday fly fishing I have turned over a wet rock, grabbed a slithering hellgrammite, hooked it under the collar, tossed it into a likely run, and caught the biggest trout of the day. These little wigglers are so tough on a hook that one may take several fish. They are also excellent bait for smallmouth bass, walleyed pike and various pondfish. If you want to collect a few they can be carried in a can of damp rotted leaves or moss. Use small short-shanked hooks. Slip the point under the hard collar just back of the head, or hook them through the tail. The former way is best. Let them drift into holding positions as you would fish garden worms. If they reach bottom they will try to hide under rocks, so keep them drifting.

GRASSHOPPERS

Everyone knows the familiar grasshopper found in fields in summer and early fall, but not everyone realizes it is an excellent surface bait for trout, smallmouth bass and panfish. On cold mornings they can be picked off their grassy perches in fields. On warm days, when they are too active to catch that way, lay a blanket over the grass and chase the hoppers onto it. Their feet will catch in the fluff of the blanket and they can easily be picked off. Carry them in a box with a sliding cover which contains pieces of nylon stockings to which the hoppers will adhere.

The best way to hook a grasshopper is under the collar back of the neck. Use a short-shank, light-wire hook. To keep it alive on the hook, don't impale it but wrap a very small rubber band a couple of turns around its body just forward of the long hopping legs, and slip the hook's point under the bands. Chronic hopper users solder two short lengths of fine wire crossway on a hook shank, one under the point and the other farther back. Then hold the hopper on the shank with its head under the bend and twist each of the two wires together lightly around the body.

When fishing a hopper, let it drift on or just under the surface. A fly rod and a floating line are the best tackle, but you can also use spinning or spincasting gear with a floating bubble a foot or so up the line.

CRICKETS

Black or dark-brown crickets are common in summer in fields and even in damp cellars. Look for them under rocks, boards, tar paper. They can be baited with bread or crumbs. Catch, keep and hook them like grasshoppers. The harnessing method is best because they are rather fragile and easy to cast off the hook. They are excellent bait for trout, bass and pondfish.

NYMPHS

If you turn over rocks or pull up masses of rotting vegetation in a stream you'll find nymphs of various kinds and sizes. Big ones can be strung on light-wire hooks or can be hooked back of the head. The wire harness can also be used with very small hooks. These nymphs of course eventually emerge to shuck their nymphal skins to transform themselves into flying insects. Some, like the stonefly nymph of western waters, grow very large and are greatly favored as baits. Those who want to study nymphs and to dress artificials to represent them will find many excellent books on the subject. Suffice it to say here that any that are big enough to put on a hook make excellent baits for trout, smallmouth bass and many other species of fish. Carry them for fishing in a small box containing damp moss or leaves.

MEALWORMS AND GRUBS

Catalpa worms, found in season on catalpa trees in the South, are popular baits for bluegills and other pondfish, and they are typical of many worms, caterpillars and grubs which can be strung on light wire hooks to catch trout, smallmouth bass and various pondfish. The white grubs of the June bug and the Japanese beetle are frequently found while digging in the garden. Fishermen hard up for bait should notice the round galls on dry goldenrod stalks. When split open, they usually yield a small grub.

I have found that smooth-skinned caterpillars are good bait, but not furry ones. Perhaps their fur or taste repels fish.

SALAMANDERS

In summer we find small salamanders in the wet leaves and rocks beside lakes and streams. I have never been successful with them, but others consider them excellent bait. Hook them through a rear thigh rather than through the tail. The tail comes off easily, but they can grow a new one.

CUT BAIT

Finally, when we've caught a fish or two, let's remember that strips of belly and even the fins make good bait, on a plain hook or on a spinner, wobbler, jig or plug. Just cut a strip of fish belly of appropriate size and hook it at one end. The strips can be cut in various shapes; it's fun to experiment.

11

How to Choose and
Use Weighted Artificial Lures

Weighted artificial lures include jigs, plastic worms (often used with jigs), plugs of many kinds, spinners for casting or trolling, spoons (which can be baited or jigged) and the time-honored pork-rind lures used for casting and for adding enticement to other terminal tackle. Many of these weighed artificials have been mentioned in previous chapters; now we'll learn more about when and how to use them to make fish strike.

HOW TO TEMPT FISH WITH JIGS

Jigs were originally devised for salt water, but they work well in fresh water, too. In fact, freshwater anglers should take a few tips from their saltwater colleagues, for jigs, properly used, will tempt nearly all freshwater gamefish. Tiny ones, even as small as ice flies, bring quick strikes from panfish. Larger ones can be fished deep for trout (including lakers), walleyes, bass and landlocked salmon.

Jigs are so named because the usual way of fishing them is by jiggling; that is, by giving them constant up and down motion much like the hops of a grasshopper, since they have little or no action of their own. They are weighted at the head to ride hook up, and therefore can be worked in dense cover with a minimum of snagging.

Jigs come in a variety of shapes. Some are bullet-headed for maximum casting distance; others are shaped like the prow of a boat, to glide easily over obstructions. The popular Fat Dart type slopes backward from top front to rear, giving it a planing action when fished downstream. Small, round-headed jigs are used for panfish. Undressed jigs, available in all sizes, shapes and colors, can be used with plastic worms or baits.

Anglers buy undressed jigs and apply their own dressings of hair, feathers, nylon and plastic skirts. They lash the dressing on with thread, winding tightly to cover the joining, secure with a whip finish, and apply lacquer to protect the thread.

When dressed jigs are ineffective, they can be "sweetened" with such diverse attractors as an end of a plastic worm, a sliver of pork rind, a pennant of balloon rubber or a strip from a lady's kid glove. A worm or other natural bait is often added to provide the enticement of scent. These should be added only as a last resort; jigs usually do well without embellishments.

Jigs with soft plastic tails come in various shapes and colors. The worm tail and the shrimp tail are two excellent examples. Most of them are flavored. Fish seem to hang on longer when they bite on the soft plastic, and the enticements of scent and taste are advantageous. Tiny jigs like these, with an inch or so of a very small plastic worm attached, are excellent lures for panfish.

Size or weight depends on the size of the fish being sought and how deep they are. Jigs for small panfish may be as tiny as $\frac{1}{32}$ of an ounce and often are dressed with a piece of plastic worm or marabou. Resting on a float or dock after swimming, one can use these little lures to tempt panfish for fun or for lunch. Others, in larger sizes, must be heavy enough to reach bottom. These average about $\frac{1}{4}$ of an ounce, but heavier ones may be needed for deep water. Use the smallest sizes or weights that will find bottom. The strike zone usually is just off bottom.

The simplest way to rig a jig—and the most effective—is to tie the jig directly to line or leader with a Loose Loop Clinch Knot. Avoid snaps or snap swivels. Use no sinkers. Small spinners sometimes are used between jig and line for added attraction, but they should be a last resort, and I have never thought they were worth anything because the attraction of scent is better.

Jigs can be rigged to anyone's choice of tackle. They fish better with the lightest line that is sensible. The rod should be stiff, particularly in the tip, to give jigs best action. The stiff tip is necessary to drive the barb home on weedless rigs.

Action is far more important than the jig's shape or color. I use three types of actions. By far the most important is the jigging or grasshoppering action which jigs were made for. In shallow water this can be merely a constant series of twitches. In deeper water, after the lure has touched bottom, raise the rod tip two or three feet, lower the tip, reel in slack until you feel the jig, and repeat the action until the jig has been fished in or until it is under the boat. If it's under the boat, give it a series of fast twitches in hope of hooking a fish which may have followed it. The second action is a slow, steady retrieve. It's not what the jig was made for, but it often works as an alternative, especially when fish are off bottom. The third action could be called "streaking," which means pumping the jig in very fast at any desired depth; sometimes the faster, the better. It is impossible to take a jig away from a fish that wants it, and this fast action may be all that is needed to make fish strike.

Methods of casting jigs vary with the type of water and whether one is fishing from shore or from a boat. Jigs can be cast, drifted or trolled as they are or with bait or another attractor attached.

From shore the jig is usually cast as far as possible and allowed to sink on a *loose line* so it will fall vertically to the bottom. If it is handled on a tight line it will swing in on a curve, thus decreasing effectiveness on the

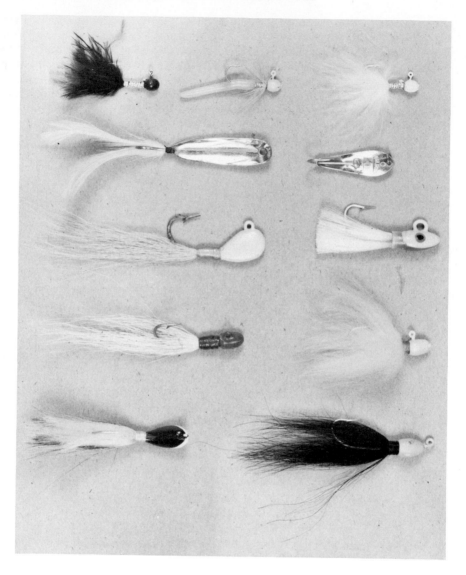

Jigs for Fresh Water

3 Thomson Doll Jigs for Panfish

Squid-type Jig   Mackerel Jig
Upperman Bucktail   Bullet-head Jig
Bullet-head, Flat-top Jig   Oval-head Jig
Spade-head Jig, Hair Tail   Round-head Jig

bottom. When it is down, put the line under control of the reel. When the line is tight, jig it in along bottom and up the slope, as has been explained.

When jigging from a boat to shore, cast the lure as close to shore as advisable, allow it to sink, and jig it in down the slope and along bottom as usual. When it is under the boat, remember to give it added twitches in case a fish has followed it in. Also jig it up for the same reason. A following fish may take it when it reaches the surface. It may be advisable to use both bow and stern anchors to keep the boat in position. Lower them very quietly.

Another jigging method is to troll slowly near structures, keeping the lure jigging actively along bottom. It may help to run the boat in reverse to permit the transom to cut the speed.

How to Fish Jigs

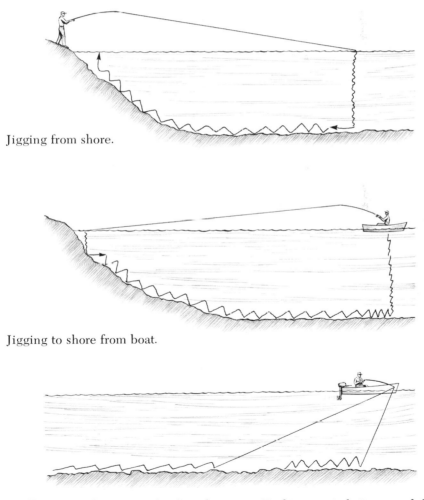

Jigging from shore.

Jigging to shore from boat.

Trolling—twitch jig actively along bottom.   Drifting—twitch jig up and down.

Jigging in streams is similar except that the current affects the lure. The usual method is to cast downcurrent with a jig that is heavy enough to touch bottom while being retrieved. An ideal weight will hang in the current just off bottom. In any case, jigging downcurrent requires less rod action because the current does most of the work.

When streams are very swift the alternative to using a jig that is too heavy is to cast upcurrent, reeling rapidly enough to keep a tight line but slowly enough to feel bottom occasionally. This is a good way to get snagged, so bring plenty of jigs!

Properly used, a jig is one of the most effective of all types of lures, and readers are urged to experiment with them. They are ineffective when the dressing becomes wrapped under the bend of the hook, so inspect the lure occasionally and be sure the dressing is separated evenly on both sides of the shank.

MORE STRIKES ON PLASTIC WORMS

There are nearly as many ways of rigging plastic worms as there are fishermen. Those who seek bass, walleyes and other bottom feeders agree that plastic worms are among the half dozen or so best lures year-round. In fact, many plastic-worm addicts won't bother with anything else. Since opinions vary on how to rig them, when to strike, and so forth, we offer our own and will mention others so readers can decide for themselves. Plastic-worm fishing is very similar to jigging, so what has been said about one applies to the other.

Plastic worms vary in size between miniatures three inches long for panfish and giants nine inches long for lunker bass and other behemoths, so six inches is a good average. Worms also vary in shape; some are smooth, others beaded, and others have spaded or forked tails. The more wormlike in appearance, the better. Some plastic worms come rigged, but experienced anglers prefer to rig their own. Nearly all colors and combinations are available, and everyone has his preferences.

For surface or near-surface fishing, a six-inch worm can be cast without weight. A weedless one can be cast to lily pads or into grassy channels and allowed to slither over pads or obstructions. Fish in the shallows below are quick to sense surface activity and should smash the lure when it reaches openings.

For fishing in deeper water, a sinking worm or a floater with a little lead can be made to sink and swim slowly. I always use floaters to avoid rigging the wrong kind. Lead makes the head sink, and the waving tail gives the worm a lifelike action.

Big bass hide in inaccessible places. Anglers should approach quietly, cast the lure beyond the suspected lair, and bring it over the spot before letting it sink. With weedless worms, hang-ups, even in dense brush, are rarer than might be assumed. When the lure catches, try to pull it out gently because a strong pull may sink the barb into the obstruction. When a lure can't be freed, the alternatives are to put the boat over it and pull it up, or to break loose. Weedless worms can work smoothly through very dense tangles.

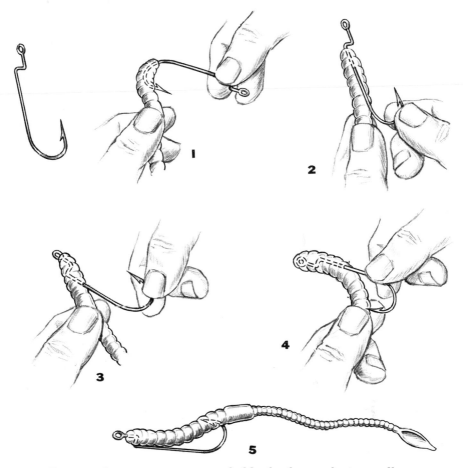

Rigging plastic worm on worm holder hook to make it weedless.

Since drop-offs are good bass structures, here are a few suggestions for fishing them: Use a nonweedless, weighted worm unless weeds and other obstructions call for a weedless one. Cast it to the water's edge and work it into the depths in short hops, with short pauses in between. As it goes deeper the hops can be longer. To do this, lower the rod to the ten o'clock position, raise it slowly while twitching the tip in short, rapid jerks, then drop it back to ten o'clock as the worm settles to the bottom. Reel in slack line as quickly as possible and repeat until the cast has been fished out. Before retrieving, dance the lure on the bottom in case a fish has followed it. The change in action may bring a strike.

Don't avoid discolored water, particularly when fishing for largemouth bass. Bass have a feeling of security when water is turbid and often feed

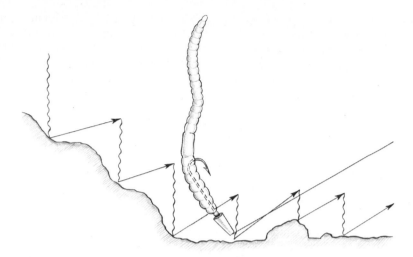

To fish weighted plastic worm properly, let worm settle to bottom, twitch it upward and forward slightly, and repeat during the retrieve. A slow retrieve is usually best, but vary speed until there's a strike.

ravenously then. Although they may not see the lure at any distance, most plastic lures are scented, so fish can smell them. These scents, incidentally, help to disguise human odor. Best results in discolored water are obtained with lures that make noise.

Even experts don't agree on when to strike with a plastic worm. The take, instead of being a strong hit, may be a gentle tap-tap-tap, indicating that the fish is mouthing the lure. One school of thought is to give line so the fish can swim for a short distance while taking in the lure; when he stops, reel in slack and strike hard.

Divers who have watched bass take plastic worms report that they often inhale them and eject them instantly. Of course this suggests the logic of striking at the slightest nibble. We might say that when you feel gentle tugs on a weedless worm, delay the strike until the fish has stopped its run. When you are using a nonweedless worm, strike instantly. In dense brush, also strike instantly—and with enough force to haul the fish out of the tangle.

Smallmouth bass hit small plastic worms hard. The worms can be fished on small jigs or with one or two split shot a foot or so up the line. White, blue or yellow are effective colors. Small, pink-headed jigs with white worms are popular for crappies, white bass and bluegills, but it pays to experiment with other colors. Panfish want the smallest jigs, rigged with a short piece of a small worm. Tackle dealers provide them for the purpose. Number 10 hooks are good choices but number 6 or 8 reduce chances of taking small fish.

I have found to my sorrow that some plastic worms react with the plastic trays in some tackleboxes, dissolving the trays and creating a mess. If in doubt, keep the two separated. Plastic worms sometimes become dry, but they work better when oily. The "Fenwick Newsletter" says to put them in a plastic bag with a few drops of Johnson's Baby Oil. This works nicely. It also suggests that when transparent worms become cloudy they can be made transparent again by leaving them in the sun for a short time. I haven't tried that.

Plastic salamanders, rigged and fished like plastic worms, are successful at times. Strike instantly at the slightest sign of a take.

TIPS ON PLUGS

Even old hands at the game sometimes become frustrated in selecting among the myriad plugs on the market, with new types being offered every day. There are chuggers, darters, divers, flashers, plunkers, poppers, rattlers, splashers, splutterers, swimmers and wobblers, in many sizes and in numerous color combinations for fishing on the surface, for floating and diving, for deep running, for bottom bumping, and more.

How do we make a reasonable selection that will tempt fish to strike under most circumstances? First, we understand that plugs fall into three divisions: surface, floating-diving and deep running. We can start with only three or four in each category, for a total of less than a dozen, in sizes or weights to suit one strength of tackle. These, wisely chosen, will suit most conditions at all depths plugs are suited to, and will provide the varied actions or sounds that tempt fish to strike.

Color combinations are also perplexing in their infinite variety. They are much less important than type. Let's start with only one color combination of each type in the middle range (as discussed in Chapter 9). Later on it will be helpful to own darker and lighter ones.

From there, novice fishermen can broaden their collection as they wish. Another strength of tackle may require another set of plugs. Added color combinations take our eye, and there are other older types we may want to try, as well as newer innovations, some of which should be regarded with suspicion. But depend on the old standbys which have been on the market for years because they have proved themselves.

Surface Plugs

Surface plugs are designed to look edible to fish even when lightly cast and allowed to sit on the water until the ripples have subsided. A fish may rise and smack the floater as soon as it alights. If this doesn't happen in productive water, you can be pretty sure fish are eyeing the offering and trying to make up their minds whether they want it for dinner. A slight twitch, followed by a pause and a few more twitches, may tempt the strike. Keep the line tight and under control. From then on, fish the plug as the manufacturer's printed instructions advise. All plugs are fished with different actions and at different speeds. Read the instructions and keep them with your plugs.

The accompanying illustration shows four reliable plugs. The Injured

Surface Plugs

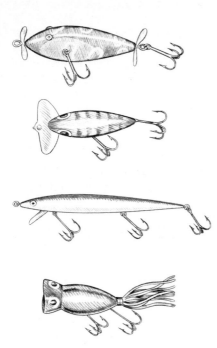

Creek Chub's Injured Minnow has propellers fore and aft for surface-splashing injured baitfish effect when retrieved steadily and slowly. It works best on calm surfaces.

Arbogast's Jitterbug has a cupped metal lip protruding from each side to make it wobble with a plopping sound when reeled slowly or erratically. It is good on a calm surface or during mild ripples.

Rapala-type baitfish imitations are fished as a crippled minnow would act: cast to target, allow to sit until ripples cease, then make it quiver. Repeat action, pulling it under the surface periodically.

Arbogast's Hula Popper has a dished face that makes a popping sound when jerked slightly. The skirt (changeable) gives added action, especially in calm water. It is fished as above, except that it won't dive.

Minnow is typical of plugs with propellers either at head or tail or both. The revolving blades make it splutter in motion, so it works best on a fairly calm surface. After the cast-pause-twitch method just described, pull it through the water just fast enough to make the blades revolve, stopping it every few feet. Fish may strike when it moves slowly. If not, speed up the retrieve gradually. A rule is to work plugs faster in warmer water because fish are more active then, and slower in colder water for the opposite reason. Another rule is to start slowly and to gradually speed up the action until you get strikes.

The famous Jitterbug has been with us for many years. It has an excellent action. The cupped metal lip pushes the surface water, causing the plug to wobble from side to side with a plopping sound. Start with the cast-pause-twitch retrieve, then alternate steady and erratic retrieves. It also can be used as a popper.

Another plug with a very different action is one of the Rapala type. The original Rapala now has many counterparts, such as the Rebel. Start this one the same way, then give it a feeble action like a wounded baitfish. If this doesn't make fish strike the action can be speeded up. (Remember Darwin's law of the survival of the fittest. Fish, like other creatures, have an instinct to kill ill or wounded prey.)

Tackle stores offer many varieties of poppers in all shapes, sizes and colors. After starting as above, give the rod tip a slight twitch. The plug will jump and push water ahead of it because of its concave head, thus making a slight pop. This adds the enticement of sound.

I like the Hula Popper because the plastic skirt fluffs on each pop to provide added motion, and because the skirt can be quickly changed to one of another color. Other types of poppers are dressed with tails of hair, feathers and synthetic materials. Some have small wobbling spoons as tails.

In selecting any of these lures it is better to try the smallest ones that suit the tackle. Big fish will take small lures, but small fish have trouble with big ones.

These lures are of course most suitable for bass and the pike family, but owners of spinning tackle, and even of fly rods, should try their tiny counterparts for other species of fish. Tiny plugs are deadly for big brown trout, especially during dusk or at night. They also work well for large rainbows and brook trout, as well as walleyes and Pacific species of salmon.

Many fishermen are content with surface plugs and want nothing else because they enjoy the thrill of seeing smashing strikes on top. Good surface fishing usually occurs only at certain times of day and/or at certain seasons. At least ninety percent of the time we find fish deep.

Floating-Diving Plugs

Floating-diving plugs lie on the surface at rest, but submerge on the retrieve. When line tension is released they pop back to the surface again. The action is produced by a metal or plastic lip. The depth that the plug will dive depends on the size and cant of the lip. Four different types of floater-divers are shown in the accompanying illustration.

A new type of floater-diver to appear on the market is the "alphabet plug," so named because the small manufacturers who make them call them Big O, Big N, etc. A large manufacturer who makes the famous Rebel plugs calls its version the Big R. Famous angling writer and bass expert Homer Circle likens them to golf balls with tails. They are fat, rounded floaters with large diving lips which cause them to vibrate during fast retrieves.

As this is being written alphabet plugs are earning top prizes in bass competitions. They can be popped on the surface or pulled under it, very fast retrieves making them run deep. Since one of the tricks of getting strikes is to work them near submerged brush and trees, many lures are lost. Anglers are philosophical about this because they take a lot of big bass. I don't know how they would work on other species, but it is surely worth a few tries —especially for big brown trout in deep pools.

Another, very different floater-diver is a banana-shaped plug that resembles a wounded baitfish when retrieved on the surface, and when pulled under travels with the energetic wiggle of a fat woman running for a bus. The Flatfish is an example. This violent wiggle produces mild vibrations, making it productive in somewhat murky water. With a little lead on the line, it can be trolled deep.

Third on my basic list, but not necessarily third in importance, are the sonic plugs. The position of the eye makes them dive and vibrate when re-

Floating-Diving Plugs

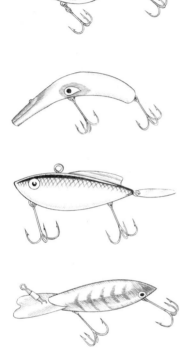

Alphabet plugs (Big O, Big N, etc.) are fat, rounded floaters with large diving lips which vibrate and make sound during fast retrieve. They can be popped, fished on surface, or pulled at various depths. Some have rattlers. Best results usually come when fished fast and deep in or near cover.

Flatfish and Lazy Ike types in proper izes can be used with any tackle. Non-sinking models float at rest and can be pulled under to provide intense wiggling action. Add split shot on line for deeper fishing.

Sonic types (Arbogast's Razorback shown here) have the eye on top. They have a vibrating sound chamber which rattles as the lure swims, are ideal for discolored water. Other prominent examples are the Pico Perch and True Shad.

The Bomber floats at rest but broad diving bill drives it deep and acts as a guard to prevent excessive hang-ups when fished in brush. All the plugs shown here are available in a wide choice of colors, and many come in various sizes.

trieved. The vibrations are intensified by a sound chamber that causes a rattle as the lure swims. Some versions have several eye positions to allow a selection of hook-ups for near-surface or deep fishing. Select one or two in colors similar to prevalent baitfish, and perhaps a lighter and darker one for different water and weather conditions.

Another valuable floater-diver is exemplified by the well-known Bomber, which fishes tailfirst and dives deeply because of its broad diving bill that skids the lure over obstructions. We can pull this plug down deep, pause a moment to let it rise a bit, and continue in this manner to cover a wide range of depth. It comes to the surface when tension is released; thus it has the characteristics of a floater-diver and of a deep-running plug.

Deep-Running Plugs

Some deep-running plugs are called bottom-bumpers, but of course this depends on the depth of the bottom. In my opinion, bottom-bumpers are lures made to fish on the bottom, such as plastic worms and jigs. A deep-runner which could be called a bottom-bumper is Arbogast's Mud Bug, somewhat similar in shape to a crayfish. It is available in many colors, of which Dick Kotis, who makes it, currently prefers chartreuse. By this we see that Dick seeks the middle ground in color selection. He is one of America's greatest anglers, particularly for largemouth bass. The Mud Bug contains a sound chamber that makes it ideal for deep fishing or for fishing shallow but murky water.

A Rapala-type lure for deep fishing is the Countdown, a wounded minnow type that sinks at a steady rate, so its depth can be estimated by counting seconds. If you want to fish just over bottom, count until it touches; then, on the next cast, count a few seconds less. After a partial retrieve it can be allowed to sink again. It is a good lure to use when fish are suspended.

The Hot Spot is a sonic lure that sinks, and can be handled like a Rapala. Rattling metal is enclosed for added sound, making it an excellent lure for discolored water.

Our final example among deep-runners is the famous Creek Chub Pikie. Like all lures of this type, it is a seductive wiggler, but it has no im-

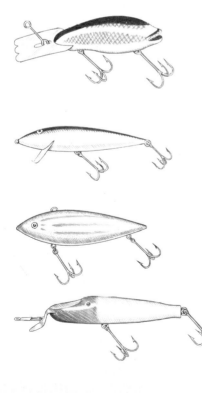

Deep-Running Plugs

Arbogast's Mud-Bug is a deep-running bottom-bumper that somewhat resembles a crayfish. The long bill and eye arrangement is typical of plugs for deep fishing. A built-in sound chamber makes it ideal for murky water.

The Countdown Rapala is a minnow imitation that sinks about a foot per second, so its depth can be estimated and the retrieve started at the proper time. It can be fished just off bottom with a fast quivering action, but all lures shown here will snag in brush.

The Hot Spot is a sonic sinker of the shad imitation type with a fast quivering action and loose shot enclosed to provide rattle. Fish it steadily or alternate a fast retrieve with pauses to let it sink.

Creek Chub's Pikie is a favorite wiggler with the typical deep-diving lip. Since it provides minimum sound, it is most productive in clear water.

portant sonic properties. The Pikie and similar lures are all-round favorites except in discolored water.

To get these lures running deep, use a fast retrieve, hauling back on the rod at intervals to make the plug dart frantically. In fishing a deeply plunging shoreline, cast a floating deep-diver near shore, let it sit a few seconds, twitch it a few times, and then retrieve it fast so it dives (and perhaps bumps) down the slope. If a floating deep-diver snags on the descent, give slack line to free the lure and allow it to rise to the surface. These lures can be used to locate submerged weed beds, mounds or other bottom structures. One quickly learns how deep each lure runs at various speeds.

A discussion of plugs wouldn't be complete without recommending the soft plastic ones. Burke Fishing Lures offers an excellent assortment of shapes, sizes and colors for various purposes. A fish can mouth them without realizing it has made a fatal mistake—until it's too late. Some of these soft plastic lures are scented. Whether the scent attracts fish is debatable, but it does conceal human odor.

FOOLING FISH WITH SPINNERS

Spinners for casting or trolling attract gamefish by flash and sound. Fishermen often buy and use them haphazardly, not realizing that they must be selected and fished properly.

Among the many and varied types of blades used for spinners, a few stand out. All are attractors whose whirling glint seems to simulate the flash of baitfish. In addition, they emit throbbing sound, perhaps imperceptible to humans, but so clearly heard by fish that they seek and strike at it even when the spinners can't be seen clearly in discolored water. The throbbing effect seems most pronounced in spinners which revolve at the greatest angle to the lure's shaft.

The most active throbber I have found is the Williams Firefly Spinner sold by the Williams Gold Refining Company, of Fort Erie, Canada. It is a fairly heavy, flat blade of blunted willowleaf shape with a groove or hump pressed into it along the center line. This causes the blade to revolve at nearly a right angle to the shaft with maximum throbbing effect. For this reason it is very popular for deep trolling. Lake trout hear it in the murky depths and are attracted to the sound even though they can't see the lure. Although this heavy, grooved, flat blade looks somewhat like the light, concave willowleaf, the characteristics of the two are entirely opposite.

Next in importance in throbbing effect is the thin Colorado blade when it is used as a spinner. The Mepps lure has a blade of this type. This egg-shaped, concave blade is often rigged on a ring, usually attached to a swivel, to make it flutter instead of spin. When it is rigged to spin it revolves at nearly 45 degrees from the shaft to provide moderate sound pulsations and considerable flash.

The well-known Indiana blade is also thin and concave, but a little longer. It spins at an angle of only about 15 degrees from the shaft, producing faint sound pulsations but considerable flash. These light, concave blades spin actively under minimum pull or current pressure.

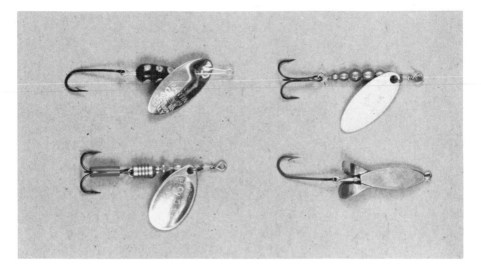

Spinners for Casting

Panther Martin   C. P. Swing
Mepps   Orvis Flat Spinner

The opposite of the Williams blade is the willowleaf—long, narrow and pointed. It spins close to the shank, provides minimum sound pulsations, but considerable flash. It is a clear-water blade whose long shape and narrow spin most accurately simulates the appearance of baitfish.

Three others are notable here. The propeller blade rotates on a shaft through its center and thus is one of the noisiest ones. For this reason it is popular on plugs because it provides sound, flash and splash or splutter. The Figure 4 and the June Bug are rigged to rotate on a wire shaft which runs through a hole in the head and through a brace extending from the underside. Thus the angle of spin is fixed at about 40 degrees or so, the blades providing average pulsations and considerable flash.

Shapes, weights and curvatures present problems in physics we don't need to bother with here. The important point is to use blades that provide the desired amount of noise or throb coupled with the amount of flash that seems needed to attract fish and to get strikes under various water conditions. Let's look at the C. P. Swing spinner as an example. This was a famous killer in the early days of spinning and is equally good now, but it has been obscured by the profusion of other types. Its willowleaf-like blade spins close to the shank for minimum throb but considerable flash with a very baitlike appearance when in motion. It is not heavy, so it sinks slowly. We would select it primarily for near-surface fishing in fairly clear water. Spinning lures that are heavier in proportion to their size and that have widely revolving blades would be better for deeper fishing.

The colors of blades are less important. Silver may be preferable for dull days and deep or murky water and brass or copper for brighter conditions, but this also depends on the amount of flash they provide. A bright

Popular Spinner Blades and Their Actions

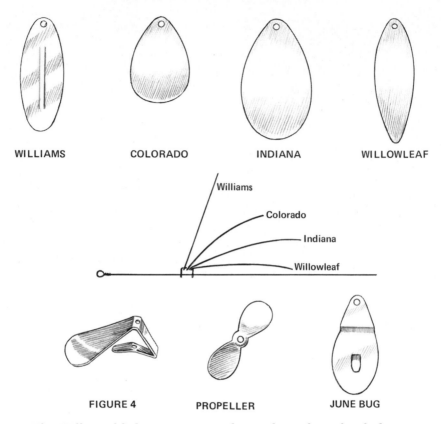

WILLIAMS   COLORADO   INDIANA   WILLOWLEAF

FIGURE 4   PROPELLER   JUNE BUG

The Williams blade rotates at nearly a right angle to the shaft, provides intense vibration but little flash. The Colorado blade revolves at nearly 45 degrees, provides minor throbbing effect and considerable flash. The Indiana blade whirls at an angle of about 15 degrees, gives little more than flash. The Willowleaf blade spins nearly parallel to the shaft, provides little water resistance and almost no vibration. The others revolve at fixed angles to the shaft, provide surface splash and flash, plus underwater flash and vibration.

blade reflecting sunlight can be so bright that it will repel rather than attract. Some blades are partially black for this reason. Other colors may be mainly for identification or decoration. It does no harm to let blades tarnish. We may want them that way on sunny days. They can be polished quickly with a piece of crocus cloth.

How to Fish Spinners
In lake fishing an erratic retrieve usually works better than a steady one. Cast and let the spinner sink on just enough loose line so it will drop to the level where the fish should be. Fish it in with a few cranks of the reel handle,

Fishing a spinning lure in a pool. When trout are resting in this pool, they usually lie between submerged rocks, which are particularly noticeable in the two spots marked *R*. When the photo was taken, trout were feeding along the left current edge and in the deepest part of the pool. Angler would cover the pool between the left current edge and the right bank, starting at position *A* and working downstream to the submerged rocks at lower left of photo. He would make several casts beyond the edge and allow lure to swing in the current, reeling in, if necessary, to keep it active. Then he would move to position *B* and cover all productive water in the pool.

let it flutter down, and repeat. Or raise the rod two or three feet, drop it back to let the spinner settle, and quickly regain slack line.

In stream fishing in shallow water the rod tip should be kept high to keep the spinner off bottom. In deeper water best results are obtained by casting quartering upstream and across. Let the spinner sink to the desired level. Then keep the blade throbbing while the current carries the lure downstream. Always plan casts, or the travel of the spinner, to direct it to good holding positions. In mild current we may do better to cast cross-stream or quartering downstream. When fish are not showing, the object is to work the lure so it just ticks bottom.

Spinning lures are excellent for discolored water, during or after a rain, when fish are on the feed. They are relatively ineffective when fish are surface feeding, because then fish prefer insects or nymphs to baitfish.

Remember the value of tiny spinning lures with fly rods or ultralight spinning tackle. When strikes are few it often helps to "sweeten" the hook with a worm, a light, slim pork-rind strip or some other artificial flutterer such as a pennant cut from balloon rubber.

The Marvelous Safety-Pin Lures

Many northerners, including this writer, have failed to appreciate safety-pin lures because of their unusual appearance. They are deadly for bass, pike, walleyes, trout and many other gamefish; in fact, many say they are second only to the properly fished plastic worm. The top arm of the safety-pin-like harness is fitted with one or more light spinners as shown in the illustration. The lower arm of the wire is hitched to an artificial weighted lure of some sort, many having colorful plastic skirts which usually are interchangeable. Since single hooks ride barb up, like a jig, this lure can be cast into tangles with minor danger of snagging. Treble hooks often are weedless. Weights usually are between a quarter and a half ounce. A strip of pork rind, a worm, shrimp tail or other bait is often added to the hook. The line is attached to the loop at the apex of the arms, without a snap. The lure won't twist line; it can be cast or trolled, and usually rides over obstructions without difficulty.

Safety pins can be fished deep or on the surface. For surface fishing, the retrieve is started immediately so the spinners flop along with a flashing, wriggling motion. An alternative is to retrieve the bait just under the surface, or a bit farther down. Let it sink a bit, reel it steadily for a few feet, let it sink again, and keep repeating the action. It is well to experiment between steady retrieves and the retrieve-and-pause method.

These lures can be worked up or down drop-offs in the manner one would fish a jig. Cast to the thin water of a drop-off, let the lure settle, raise the rod two or three feet to pull the lure off the incline, let it settle again, and so forth. In fishing up a drop-off cast out as far as possible and give the lure time to settle. When it touches bottom raise the rod tip about three feet just fast enough to feel the spinners turning. Drop the rod tip while reeling in slack, and keep repeating.

When fishing along bottom, let the lure sink as far as desired, pull it up and in as just described, and repeat several times. Then start a slow, deep retrieve just fast enough to be sure the spinners are turning.

Spinners for Trolling

Trolling spinners are usually clevised to stiff wire with a loop at the head of the wire and a fastener at the rear for attaching leader, hook or lure. A few varieties, usually using blades of the Colorado type, may be strung on linkages with split rings to make them flutter instead of revolve. Since all these are very common they need little comment.

Sizes of trolling spinners are usually selected to suit the bait and tackle. Selections of blades and their colors have been explained. We have observed that strongly throbbing spinners are preferable when trolling deep or in discolored water, and these usually are in the larger sizes.

HOW TO INCREASE STRIKES WITH WOBBLING SPOONS

A wobbling spoon is basically a spinner blade with a hook at the wide end and a means of connecting it to the line on the other, the result being that it wobbles or flutters rather than spins.

In near-surface fishing, castable wobbling spoons are handled the same as spinners except that they can be retrieved more erratically. If a spinner

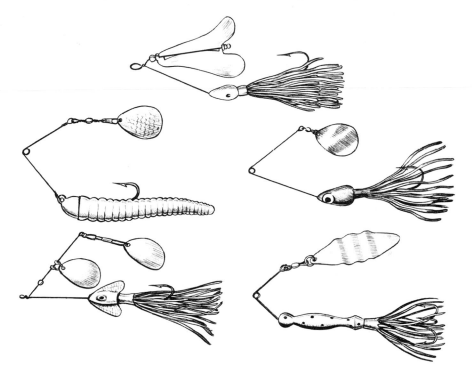

Buzzing, flashing, wriggling safety-pin lures are especially good for bass. The heavier lure rides underneath, the lighter spinner on top. The lure can be spluttered on the surface, wiggled underneath, allowed to sink to bottom and retrieved like a jig.

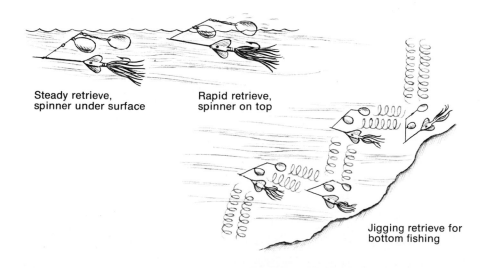

Steady retrieve, spinner under surface

Rapid retrieve, spinner on top

Jigging retrieve for bottom fishing

doesn't seem to get the results it should, try a wobbling spoon. If the spoon doesn't work, try a bit of bait or a flutterer on the hook. When that fails, you may be fishing in the wrong place or at the wrong time or at the wrong depth. If you're fishing over feeding fish, the simple wobbling spoon, with nothing added to it, can be deadly.

Thick, compact spoons can be used as jigs in water from fifteen to forty feet deep; that is, at the deep comfort zone of whatever fish we are seeking. Mark the line for that depth, cast the spoon that far, and work it with a mild bucktailing motion until it completes its dropping arc and is under the boat. Fish should take it as it flutters down but, since one or more may be following it, it should be jigged actively before retrieving, and also during the retrieve. It may draw strikes at any time. When it doesn't, try adding bait or a flutterer to the hook. Drifting over a good area while using a spoon in this manner can be very effective. Roundish spoons can be alternated with longer ones. When silver or brass don't work, try a spoon with a mother-of-pearl finish, or an enameled one like the famous Dardevle.

A place where wobbling spoons shouldn't be cast is over shallow weed beds, which are favorite abodes for Northern pike. The spoons will hang up or catch grass in such places. A surface plug or a floating-diver is better.

Spoons are very effective when trolled, with or without embellishments. Various weights seek different depths, which can be varied by boat speed. Trolling too fast will cause many of them to spin. The proper speed is when they merely flutter at the right depth.

Thin, long, light spoons are ideal for deep trolling. Try them on a weighted line with a long leader, or perhaps on an unweighted line with the proper amount of lead set as far away from the lure as possible. This is a very productive rig for all the trouts and salmons which legally can be caught that way because the long fluttering spoon is an excellent imitation of a baitfish in distress.

PORK-RIND BAITS

Among the most venerable of all weighted artificials is the pork-rind lure, usually sold in jars in a salt solution. Made from the skin of the animal, these lures are so tough that one is as good as ever even after many catches. Uncle Josh Bait Company, of Fort Atkinson, Wisconsin, is the principal manufacturer. A few examples and typical ways of using pork rind as baits and attractors are illustrated.

The time-honored method of catching bass and pickerel was to skitter a pork-rind lure on a weedless hook among lily pads and weed beds and around stumps and logs, working the lure across the surface in short, frantic spurts. It still is so today in many places.

We have spoken of "sweetening" jigs, spoons, spinners and plugs with pork-rind strips or something similar. This provides added action when the lure itself doesn't seem to be doing well enough. Don't overdo this embellishment. If one thin wiggler helps to get strikes, the addition of another one or two may cancel the advantage.

One of the best of all lures for bass, walleyes and members of the pike family is the jig and eel, which hasn't yet received proper appreciation in

Wobbling Spoons

Pearl on Copper
Mr. Champ
Wob-L-Rite
Orvis Long Spoon
Orvis Broad Spoon
Orvis Normal Spoon
Pearl on Copper, Indiana

Daredevle
Luhr Jensen
Johnson Spoon
Sidewinder
Williams Firefly
All-Pearl
Mooselook

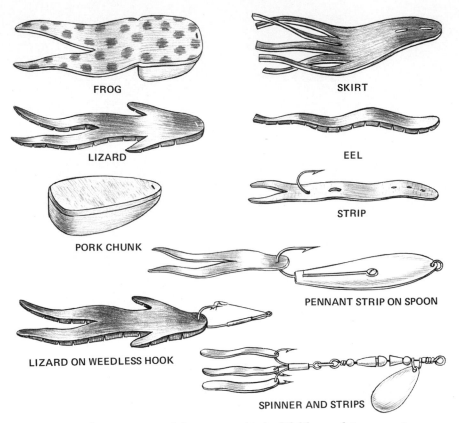

FROG

SKIRT

LIZARD

EEL

PORK CHUNK

STRIP

PENNANT STRIP ON SPOON

LIZARD ON WEEDLESS HOOK

SPINNER AND STRIPS

Pork-rind attractors and baits are tough, lifelike and inexpensive. They're available in many colors, shapes and sizes. Some are lures themselves; others act as attractors on jigs, spoons, and spinners.

this book. Merely fasten an eel-shaped pork rind to the hook of a bucktail jig and jig it on or near bottom. I like black best for deep fishing, but other colors of rind are available for jigs of any color combination. Plastic eels are also very popular for this purpose.

A lure such as the famous Johnson Silver Spoon with a pork strip attached is excellent for jigging. The weedless spoon is ideal for fishing lily pad or grassy areas. Cast to the pads and twitch it over them into open water. A bass or pickerel should be there to meet it.

Pork strips can be rigged to thwart short-striking fish. The rind is so tough that a trail hook can be set into it, as shown in the illustration. If the fish doesn't get the leading hook it should be caught on the trailer.

Let's remember, however, that the salt solution in which pork rinds are kept can rust a tacklebox if any of it is spilled. Carry pork rinds in a separate container, and wash lures before putting them back.

12

How to Select and Fish Fly-Rod Artificials

More has been written about fly fishing during the past five hundred years than about any other sport. Much of this literature gives the impression that catching fish on artificial flies is a complicated art requiring years of practice, abnormal skill, expensive equipment and vast knowledge. Let's correct that impression by saying that anyone with passable equipment who can cast thirty feet can catch fish on artificials. Thirty feet isn't very far, and more fish are caught inside this range than outside it. We don't need many flies as long as we have a variety of sizes. All that's needed to get strikes is to drift wet or dry flies over good holding positions. We won't hook as many big ones as the experts do, but we'll catch fish and have fun.

Many anglers try to perfect their technique, carefully selecting patterns on the basis of a knowledge of entomology, seasonal hatching sequences, and so on. Part of the fun of fly fishing is that it is a sport which can be carried to infinite extremes. Hundreds of books have been written about all this. Here, let's give the main points a short review and offer some suggestions on fishing the main types of fly-rod artificials. Let's start with streamers and bucktails on the assumption that fishing with them is easiest. Then we'll proceed to wet flies, nymphs, and dry flies, concluding with bass bugs and similar attractors.

STREAMERS AND BUCKTAILS

Gamefish take these long flies because they think they are baitfish, but also out of anger, curiosity, or in the spirit of play. To learn how to fish them, lie on a dock and watch baitfish as they dart about, turning and grubbing along the bottom to show their shimmering sides while searching for food. Note their actions, their colors and their shapes. Try to imitate these in fishing.

While doing this we should quickly come to the conclusion that most streamers and bucktails purchased commercially are overdressed, pleasing anglers more than the fish. This is not to say that correctly dressed old stand-bys such as the Gray Ghost, the Supervisor and the Black Ghost, for example, aren't as effective as they always were. It is to say that slimmer patterns on many occasions may be better. There are exceptions. The Muddler Minnow, which simulates a little bottom-feeder called the cockatush minnow, or sculpin, is a fat fly which also is taken as a nymph or, when floating, as a grasshopper. Few minnow imitations are as versatile.

These flies should also be about the same size as prevalent baitfish, but since schools may include baitfish of various sizes, this isn't of major importance. Use small ones on bright days in clear water, and big ones when water is high or discolored so gamefish can see them more easily.

When conditions are bright and clear, many anglers use miniature streamers or bucktails—extremely slim, and only an inch or two long. In dull colors and while drifting or being fished slowly, these may often be taken for nymphs.

Streamers and bucktails fall into two classes—imitators and attractors. The imitators, such as the Pin Smelt, Black Nosed Dace and Sidewinder, are dressed in specific baitfish coloration, and they usually are the best ones to select. The attractors, such as the Mickey Finn, Royal Coachman and Black Ghost, are brighter colored with little or no resemblance to baitfish. While they are primarily dark day and/or dirty water flies, they are also taken by feeding fish under other conditions. Fish often rise to investigate them without taking. When this happens, switch to an imitator of the same size and work the fly over the fish again.

When a fish rises to a fly it moves forward as well as upward, and then settles back into its holding position. Cast upstream of where the fish was seen so the fly has time to work into the fish's cone of vision at the proper depth.

Breather-type streamers and bucktails are important alternatives when different action seems needed to coax fish to strike. There are two types. One is either a streamer or a bucktail whose wing is divided to splay outward and backward in the form of a "V." Bucktail wings are divided by winding the thread in a figure-8 around the bases of both halves. Streamer wings are divided by selecting two pairs of feathers, each with opposite curve, and setting them on the hook back to back. The second type is the marabou streamer, a favorite killer for all gamefish when used in waters where it can be made to pulsate. Here again it should not be overdressed. The wing needn't be divided because the fluffy marabou fibers offer sufficient action of their own.

All breather-type streamers or bucktails should be made to pulsate, rather than merely pulling them in the current. They work best when given slight action on a drift or when fished slowly in quiet water. When the lie of a fish is known and it won't take anything else, rest the fish a bit and then fluff a breather-type fly nearby. If the action doesn't make the fish take from hunger, it often will do so because of anger or curiosity. These flies are particularly effective on large brown trout. A very dark one, a very light one and one of medium coloration should be sufficient in two or three sizes.

Weedless Streamers and Bucktails
The accompanying drawing shows two ways to make a fly hook weedless. One is to use Keel hooks, readily available from tackle stores and mail-order houses. In dressing the body, take care to have the center of gravity there so the hook's bend will ride upward. The wing is dressed on the forward horizontal part of the hook so it encloses the barb. Keel flies in various sizes and patterns for fresh or salt water are available commercially. These flies can be cast into brush or weeds and dragged over lily pads and branches with rare hang-ups. When they first became available, I had some doubts about their hooking ability, but these seem to be unfounded. While hooking ability may be slightly inferior to conventional hooks, this is more than balanced by their excellence in negotiating weedy spots.

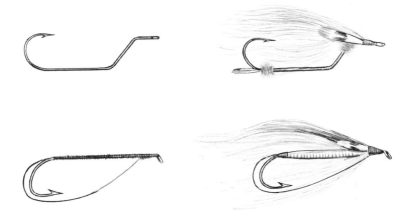

Two ways of tying a weedless bucktail or streamer fly. Top, with a Keel hook that rides with the point upright within the wings of the fly. Below, with a length of stiff monofilament tied into the dressing, bent around the barb and tied into the head.

Conventional flies can be made weedless with a short piece of mono-filament of suitable stiffness. When winding thread to start the body, wind it around both shank and monofilament, leaving a few inches of the mono-filament protruding at the tail. Dress the body as usual. Bend the monofila-ment around and slightly outside of the hook's bend and barb and tie it in at the head. Finish the dressing in the usual way. The diameter or stiffness of the monofilament of course varies with the size of the fly. Use stiff mate-rial, if possible, and remember that it will soften somewhat when wet. This weedguard is almost invisible and can be concealed entirely by the under-body.

Weighted Streamers and Bucktails
Since gamefish are usually lying and feeding close to the bottom, we must use flies which will sink. Even fast-sinking lines may not get flies to drag

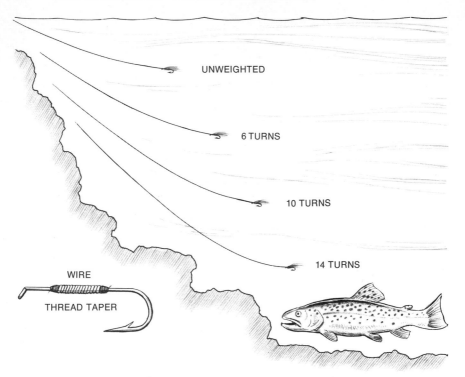

UNWEIGHTED

6 TURNS

10 TURNS

14 TURNS

WIRE

THREAD TAPER

Weighted bodies get streamers down to the fish. The hook shank is wound tightly with #22 soft copper wire or lead fuse wire, tapered at each end with tying thread. Between six and fourteen turns, depending on depth and current, are average.

bottom in fast currents. Weighting leaders or flies, or both, is often necessary. When weighting leaders, it is preferable to use several tiny split shot or lead strips rather than one large sinker. The shot or strips can be clamped to the leader just above one of the knots. Since this doesn't add to casting pleasure, weighted flies are a better solution. Use no more weight than necessary, and avoid confusion by segregating weighted patterns from unweighted ones in your flybox. One way is to dress or paint the heads in a different color.

Lead fuse wire is available where fly dressing materials are purchased. Its diameter is rated in amperes, one ampere wire having a diameter of .015 inches. This, or number 22 soft copper wire, should suffice except for very large flies which might call for two or three ampere wire. Wind the wire tightly in close coils on the middle of the shank, leaving plenty of room at head and tail for dressing. Wire ends are secured and tapered with thread. Between six and fourteen turns of wire are usually used on streamers and bucktails, depending on the diameter of the wire and the amount of weight desired. Tubular Mylar, with the core removed, is often used to cover the wire, but most types of body dressings are appropriate.

How to Make Fish Strike Streamers and Bucktails

A streamer or bucktail should be fished as a minnow swims—lazily turning while feeding on the bottom; drifting with the current; slowly swimming upstream, or suddenly darting away in panic. Four methods follow. We can experiment to find what works best at the time, and one can be combined with another. Fish often strike bucktails viciously, but sometimes they have to be teased into striking. Teasing works best when the lie of a big one is known.

The *swing retrieve* is used so often that many anglers don't realize there are others. Cast quartering upstream in a mild current, cross-stream in an average one, and quartering downstream when the flow is fast. First casts are made nearby and subsequent ones gradually extended to work the fly along feed lanes and into promising holding positions. As the fly works downstream it travels across the current. No tip action is needed in fast current, but some is when the current is mild to slow. If swift current causes the line to bag downstream, use upstream mends to keep the fly from whipping. When no surface action is noted the fly must travel as deeply as possible. This is accomplished by casting upstream and across, by using a sinking line, by weighting the fly or leader, or by a combination of these methods. Keep the rod pointed at the fly and keep it low unless raising it is necessary to guide the fly through shallow water. Action is given when necessary by raising and lowering the rod tip. Try to make the

The swing retrieve quartering downstream. This slick behind a large rock in a riffle would be covered by casting to position A so the fly would swing close to the rock and through the slick, whose edges are marked by the dashed lines. Following casts to positions B, C and D should cover the area properly. On completion of each swing, the fly will hang downstream, and should be jigged actively before retrieving it by the hand-twist method.

Cross-stream casting to a slower current. We want to drift a streamer or bucktail close to the shoreline without drag. To do this, we would cast directly across stream to point *A* and release and mend line between points *A* and *B*. At point *B* the line has extended quartering downstream, where the deeply sunken fly will start to swing. Hold the rod tip very low, even dunking it, during the retrieve, *X* to keep the fly deep.

fly swing at moderate speed, give it action when necessary, and guide it into places that look productive while keeping it as deep as possible.

When the fly has completed its swing it hangs downstream. This is the time to give it prompt and vigorous action because fish often follow a fly and will take it when its action changes. Work it for fifteen seconds or so by raising and lowering the rod tip. Recover it by the hand-twist retrieve.

In the *hand-twist retrieve* the cast is made directly downstream, or nearly so. This retrieve is made by turning the fingers of the line hand to collect small loops progressively in its palm as line is recovered. The action of the fly is supposed to imitate the slow progress of a baitfish working against the current. Line can be taken in and let out as desired to explore good holding positions.

This retrieve is excellent when the fly is cast downstream to swing in along an undercut bank or to maneuver it into spots like active eddies, near-shore edges and fallen trees in the water.

A breather-type fly such as a marabou pattern or a splaywing does well in such places. If we presume that a large trout should be lying in a spot such as a hole under an undercut bank, and if it doesn't strike by ordinary methods, it can often be teased into doing so. Work the fly into the position and keep it fluffing there for as long as it takes to smoke a cigarette; a minute or two. Nothing may happen for a while but a savage strike may occur suddenly, perhaps because the fly has made the fish angry. I have taken many big trout by this method.

This retrieve also is valuable when fan-casting from a boat on a pond or lake, particularly in an inlet where a current is running. When there is no current it may be preferable to recover the fly by slow stripping because this makes it more active.

The *panic strip* is another teasing way to use a streamer or bucktail, especially valuable when other methods don't produce and a fish is seen or is presumed to be in a certain location. Cast up and across current a bit beyond the position. Work the fly in front of it and then suddenly strip it in fast. The impression presumably given is that the lure suddenly sees the fish and flashes away in panic. Make a down and across current cast in the same way and skitter or jerk the fly as close to the fish as possible. The panic strip seems to tempt fish to smash the lure only because it is trying to escape.

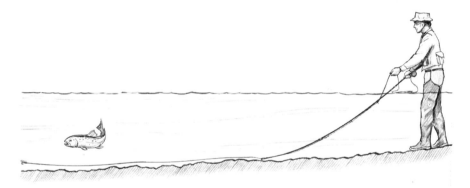

One way to be sure the fly is deep enough is to submerge the rod tip and retrieve the fly as shown above. Retrieving with the rod held high pulls the fly off the bottom.

The *dead drift* cast will remind Atlantic salmon anglers of the "greased line method" because it is so similar. It works best in moderate flow, such as in a large pool. Cast upstream and across to let the fly run deep. The fly will drift crossways of the current and should be kept doing so at current speed. When the line bags downstream, causing the fly to speed up and start to whip, the line is mended upstream as often as is necessary. If the fly slows down it can be speeded up by mending the line downstream, thus bagging it a bit. In this way, the fly is kept drifting at moderate speed by mending the line one way or the other. At the same time, keep the fly active by giving the rod tip action when necessary.

While streamers and bucktails will take big fish all season long, they are particularly effective when fished deep and slowly during the run-offs of early spring when trout are lying on bottom and feeding there. Larger sizes with considerable glint are seen best when streams in spring are high and discolored. If we fish the fly at the proper level in the manner that a baitfish swims we should be confident of success. When using sinking lines also use shorter leaders so the current won't sweep the fly up.

Although many streamers and bucktails made for trout also will take smallmouth and largemouth bass, bass have favorites that are somewhat different. Largemouth flies may have to be weedless. I have had excellent success with large, floppy multicolored streamers dropped crudely with a *splat*, allowed to sit on the surface a few moments, and then pulled under and fished in. Wooly Worms and Muddlers do well and can be fished in the same manner. Breather-type patterns such as marabous and splaywings also are excellent.

MORE STRIKES WITH WET FLIES

Wet flies imitate winged insects which have drowned and are drifting in the current or which remain alive and are weakly trying to swim. Wet flies may imitate nymphs which have hatched into winged flies underwater just before emergence, or they may simulate winged flies of mayfly and caddis types which go underwater to lay eggs. Wet flies on occasion may also be taken for tiny baitfish, or unhatched nymphs.

Wet flies are the most venerable of all artificials. They were employed long before Dame Juliana Berners wrote about them in the fifteenth century and also before Charles Cotton added his section to Walton's *Compleat Angler* in the seventeenth. Early in this century the advent of streamers and bucktails, and of dry flies and nymphs, relegated them to the background. This is a pity because modern tackle makes them more effective than ever. Many of us of the older generation learned fly fishing with them. They offer an extremely efficient way to take trout and other species which feed on insects.

The classic way to fish wet flies was to fasten three flies to a leader, making what was known as a "cast". This method is still popular in the British Isles. One is the point fly, at the end of the leader. The other two are dropper flies, tied to leader extensions between point and butt.

How to Tie a Leader with Droppers

To do this in the modern manner, start with about twenty inches of leader butt and tie in the next section about twelve inches down it, using the usual Blood Knot. Do not trim off the eight inches or so of monofilament which protrudes from the knot because this is a dropper to which a fly will be attached. The section tied in also is about twenty inches long and the next section is tied in in the same way, also leaving about 8 inches of the heavier monofilament for a second dropper. The point fly can be tied to the end of this final section, or a tippet can be added between them.

The object is to separate the dropper flies and the point fly to prevent them from tangling. This is done by spacing the droppers on the leader, by making the droppers of the stronger of the two sections of monofilament, and by keeping the droppers short. The Blood Knot permits the droppers to extend at right angles to the leader. Flies are tied to droppers with the Turle Knot. (I first put an Overhand or Wind Knot in the end of the monofilament and then fasten the fly with the Turle Knot, working the two knots together, as added insurance against slipping.)

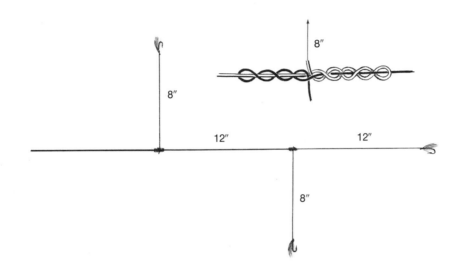

How to tie a leader with droppers. Each dropper is an unclipped end of the heavier section of monofilament which extends from the Blood Knot, shown in close-up just before it is pulled tight. Flies are tied to droppers and point with the Turle Knot.

Casting Methods with Wet Flies

Since wet flies simulate dead insects, or live ones barely moving, they are usually drifted in currents or fished slowly in currentless water. Casts are planned to direct the flies through holding positions or feeding lanes, at the level of the fish, which normally is close to bottom.

My favorite method of fishing wet flies in streams is the *dead drift,* as used with streamers, except that little, if any, action is given to the flies. The current does the work. Cast upstream and across to let the flies run deep and mend the line, upstream or downstream as necessary, to keep the cast at current speed. Small subcurrents work on one fly, which activates the others.

An exciting dividend when using more than one fly on a leader is that when they drift into a potential position a trout may grab one of them. Not to be outdone, another fish or two may strike the others. Conservation-minded anglers may question the ethics of multiple fly use, but we hope users will have "catch and release" in mind.

The most productive approach to this classic trout pool would be wading up the far shore. When angler arrives at *A*, he would cast up and across to point 1, allowing the fly to drift until drag sets in. Drag is postponed by upstream mends, or by checking the cast to provide some slack line. Casts would be made to points 2 and 3; then the angler would wade upstream to position *B* and continue casting to points 1, 2 and 3.

After completing the dead drift, the flies can be recovered slowly with the *hand-twist retrieve* discussed for streamers. The flies may be taken for tiny baitfish, as well as for insects. The hand-twist retrieve is also useful in currentless water, particularly when the retrieve is along the bottom. This can be alternated with a *hand strip,* jerking the flies in only two or three inches at a time to give them different activity.

Another method in currents is to *dap the rear dropper fly.* Hold the rod high with enough line out to keep the rear fly barely out of water. By twitching the rod tip, the rear fly can be made to dance over the surface, touching it occasionally, in the manner of using a dry fly. This "dapping" of the rear fly often makes trout leap out of the water for it. One of the other flies, being pulled by the current, may be taken at the same time. Fish often hook themselves.

If the cast is swinging, the rear fly can be *skittered* over the surface to provide a tiny wake.

Selecting Wet Flies
In spring, when stream temperatures are in the 50s, the best wet-fly fishing should be in the afternoon when the sun has warmed the water. Trout are usually feeding below the surface, and wet flies are productive.

Since the most popular patterns vary with the season, the region and the whim of anglers, I'll merely state two general rules here. Natural insects hatch in a succession of color changes that start with blue, gray, black and brown in early spring and gradually lighten as the season progresses. Flies like the Blue Quill, Leadwing Coachman, Dark Hendrickson, and March Brown are good producers early in the year, in sizes 12 and 14. When insect hatches occur, try to match them with one or two of the flies on the cast. Use lighter patterns later, and go to smaller flies, particularly in the low water of summer.

Late spring and summer are dry-fly times, but there are wet patterns that produce all season long. These include the Leadwing Coachman, Hare's Ear, Dark Cahill, Hendrickson, and the Black Gnat, as well as some of the light colored ones. Others I like are Wooly Worms predominantly black or brown, small Muddlers, and terrestrials such as grasshopper imitations. Try one of each type on a three-fly cast, perhaps with a seasonal favorite on the point, a lighter pattern on the lower dropper, and a terrestrial on the upper one. One may produce most of the strikes, and we can be guided by that.

While three flies on a cast may be the most popular number, some wet-fly specialists prefer only two, and many never use more than one.

My wet-fly box is filled with many old patterns with which I learned the first lesson in fly fishing as a boy. In it are many bright and gaudy flies such as the Parmacheene Belle and Yellow Sally which seemed indispensable in the old days. They rarely are used now. It also contains many imitator patterns just as good now as they were then. Times change. We have neglected wet-fly fishing in favor of modern methods. Perhaps some anglers of the new generation will appreciate its historic efficiency and charm and will restore it to popularity again. It still is an excellent way to learn!

NYMPHS

Nymph fishing, the newest of fly-rod methods, can be complicated for those who want to delve into its entomological aspects. Many successful nymph fishermen ignore most of the technical background and fish the way we'll explain here. They maintain that the nymph pattern isn't all that important because anyone who grubs around in the silt and rocks of a stream always will find dozens of varieties of nymphs in all sizes and stages of development. The idea, they think, is to select an average-size artificial nymph— perhaps a gray one—and to learn to fish it properly, because presentation is more important than pattern.

I learned the rudiments of nymph fishing many years ago, and used the only fly rod I owned at the time. It happened to have been made by Fred Thomas, in Bangor, Maine, so of course it was a very good one. I didn't realize then that it was anything very special because split-bamboo rods were customary in those days. Old Fred would have flipped in his grave if he had known I fished worms and minnows with it, and misused it in other ways, including breaking off four inches of a tip by sitting on it while riding in a float-plane. I put a tip-top on the damaged end and liked the increased stiffness better. At an early age I learned to catch trout on nymphs with it.

My favorite fishing buddy at the time seemed to be an expert at catching trout on nymphs, but he rarely used more than one pattern. We made this one by the dozen by tying small bunches of brown bucktail butts around small long-shanked hooks and cutting each bunch end short before pulling the thread to make the hair ends spin around the hook. When half a dozen or so tight applications covered the shank we whip-finished the head and trimmed the hair rather raggedly, as short as possible. This made an imitation of a caddis nymph case. We put a bit of twist-on lead a foot or so up the silkworm gut leader and drifted this creation behind rocks in streams and into other places we thought trout should be. We caught many trout, but of course they were more plentiful and less sophisticated then.

It was not unusual to cast the nymph into a pool and to put the rod down during lunch. Settled on the bottom and tethered by the bit of lead, the nymph would wiggle in minor currents in the gravel, would be investigated by many trout and often be picked up by one which would hook itself and make its predicament known. It was only in later years that I learned nymph fishing was supposed to be difficult.

Since those early days so much has been written about nymph fishing that anglers can delve into the subject in as much detail as they wish. It pays to understand nymph types and their habits, the tackle that works best, and the various presentation methods that make fish strike. At least equally important is to know the usual light take of a fish, and what to do about it.

Nymph and Their Habits

Flying insects lay eggs in streams in warm weather during the fishing season. These settle and some of them develop into larvae, and then into nymphs when their rudimentary humps, or wing pads, become visible. This may take one or more years, during which time the developing nymphs burrow in silt or clings to rocks, often becoming dislodged by currents and being eaten by fish.

Eventually, as if on nature's signal and usually when waters warm up to 50 degrees or more, the nymphs of one subspecies or another rise or swim to the surface to shed their nymphal skins, thus transforming themselves into flying insects which mate and lay eggs to repeat the process. At these times, when the various hatches occur, trout and other fish go on feeding sprees, but they devour nymphs on the bottom, or drifting with currents, whenever they can find them. This may be an oversimplification, but it should serve to show why fishing with artificial nymphs can be so successful.

Most important among these complex classifications are the various subspecies of *mayfly nymphs,* which have pronounced humps on their shoulders containing their rudimentary wings. The nymphs rise and float when ready to hatch and remain on the surface until they have shucked their nymphal skins and expanded their wings to permit them to fly. Since these mayflies drift in feed lanes, trout are waiting for them there too, and consume them avidly. Such hatches can be so obvious that they simulate a snow storm.

Next in importance is the *caddis nymph,* called the "home-builder" because it surrounds itself with a case made of sand and bits of debris held together by mucous as strong as cement. A crude deer-hair representation of this was discussed earlier, but there are much better ones. Some fishermen apply lacquer to shanks of fine-wire hooks and roll them up in a mixture of sand and pulverized bark to build up excellent imitations of these tube-like cases. Ripe caddis nymphs swim to the surface to shuck the cases and transform themselves into flies. The gravel and detritus so often found in trouts' stomachs are the remainder of these cases.

Stonefly nymphs usually are considered third in importance. They emerge like mayflies do, but crawl up on streamside rocks to shed their cases and to develop and harden their wings. Some of the stonefly nymphs are very large and fat, and the shucked cases often litter rocks along streams.

Other types include nymphs of the *dobsonfly,* the *dragonfly* and the *damselfly,* rapid swimmers which are found in backwaters.

Smallest of all these is the *midge,* a fly whose fat but tiny wormlike pupa is usually less than a quarter of an inch long. Its representation is dressed on a number 20 hook. The pupae hang in the surface film and are eagerly sipped in by trout. Where they are present, their representations, soaked in the mouth before casting, can be deadly in spite of their small size.

Readers who wish to study nymphs further can find illustrated technical information in Ernest Schwiebert's book *Nymphs* and a lot of extremely valuable angling instruction in a little book with supplementary color plates called *Compara-Hatch,* by Alfred Caucci and Robert Nastasi. It is distributed by the Cortland Line Company, of Cortland, New York 13045.

Novices who want to assemble collections of artificial nymphs shouldn't do so blindly. Ask regional experts to suggest a few of the most important types. A small variety is all that should be necessary, at least to start with. An understanding of nymphs and their emergence dates is more important than a full fly box.

Tackle for Nymph Fishing

Any rod suitable for light fly fishing will handle nymphs properly. Leaders should be nine feet or longer, tapered to 5X or 6X (about two pounds). For large nymphs, on big streams, a heavier tippet is required. Many anglers prefer tippets two or three feet long because they seem to make nymphs act more naturally. Tippets testing only two pounds or less may seem rather light to novices, but they can handle very big trout unless there are obstructions or unless too much tension is put on the fish. The alternative is to use stronger tippets and to get fewer strikes.

In nymph fishing, leaders with a minimum of knots are preferable if there is a danger of picking up bits of algae on the knots. The Cortland Line Company's Twin-Tip leaders are excellent. They come with one butt section of stiff tapered nylon and two tip sections (one being an extra) of softer tapered nylon; actually two leaders in one. They are joined by only one knot, and I add about two feet of finer level monofilament as a tippet, giving me a twelve-foot leader, which most nymph fishermen consider about average, with only two knots.

Except under early-season, high-water conditions, trout take artificial nymphs very lightly, merely by picking them up. The most important part of nymph fishing is to learn to detect these very light takes and to tighten on the fish instantly. The signal usually is a slight pull on the line. To detect this more easily, wind the line-leader joint with fluorescent floss and varnish it. Bobbers for this purpose are so light and tiny that they can be cast without difficulty, but I prefer to mark the line-leader connection with a fluorescent color. While takes may be so light that they are almost imperceptible, high water conditions may make strikes much stronger, and fish may hook themselves when nymphs are drifting in strong currents, or even when the nymph is "dead" and lying nearly motionless on the bottom or hanging on completion of a swing.

We need unweighted nymphs, usually for top-water fishing, and weighted ones for dragging bottom. Since it's difficult to tell one type from the other, it is best to keep them separated in different boxes. Unweighted nymphs can be fished on bottom if as small an amount of lead as necessary is added a foot or more up on the leader—a twist-on, or a few small well-spaced split shot. In strong currents both weighted nymphs and lead may be necessary when fish are hugging bottom. Nymphs can be weighted by applying one-ampere fuse wire (15/000 inch diameter) to the body. If nymphs are too heavily weighted they travel through the water too fast and fish don't hit them as well as when they are so slightly weighted that they sink slowly and move delicately when they are twitched.

During or just prior to an insect hatch, the best fishing may be on the surface or just below it. We can then use a floating line and a long leader. Use an unweighted nymph, moistened in the mouth, for surface or near-surface work, one slightly weighted for drifting deeper. A floating line with a sinking tip may be preferable in pools or deep runs, or for dragging bottom when streams are fairly shallow. The sinking line is a last resort in nymph fishing because drifts can't be controlled as well with it, and it is more difficult to distinguish strikes. Judge how deep you want to fish, and select the line accordingly, allowing weighted nymphs and/or lead on the leader to help control depth.

If you ever forget to bring nymphs on the stream, take a wet fly with an appropriate body—a fuzzy one like a Hare's Ear or a Coachman—and cut off the wings, leaving a small nub to represent the wing pad. Wet-fly fishing and nymph fishing have many similarities. Casting methods are much the same.

Getting Strikes on Nymphs

In early spring when streams are high and cold, anglers who prefer the fly rod with artificial flies usually think in terms of streamers or bucktails. We shouldn't neglect nymphs because many lunkers are taken on the bottom with them at this time.

The technique is quite different from usual warm-weather tactics. The trick is to roll and drift the nymph *on bottom*; right down over the gravel, because that's where the fish are, and their metabolism is too low for them to move more than inches for food. By the same token, the nymph must be fished very slowly. Work it into good holding positions, and you'll get strikes. A sinking nymph and some lead on the line are necessary. When trout are not actively feeding, depth is the secret weapon!

Under these conditions the best tactic is to cast the nymph quartering downstream and to shake out some extra line to prevent drag. Work the bottom slowly in the good holding positions. When the cast straightens out downstream, let the nymph hang there, and give it a few twitches.

When streams are lower, warmer and clearer, our tactics change. The best method is to cast upstream. The nymph can be worked along bottom with little or no drag and, since fish face upstream, it is more difficult for them to see the angler.

Upstream fishing with nymphs is tricky. We have to hold the rod fairly high and strip in line as the current washes it back. We have to be in control of the line, watching for the signal of a strike so we can react instantly. We must make the nymph drift along bottom unless there are signs of surface or near-surface feeding activity. When there are, nymphs can be fished near-surface in the same manner as wet flies.

There is no reason why nymphs can't be used near the surface in the same manner as a cast of wet flies, with one or two on droppers above the one on point. Nymphing is not entirely bottom fishing; it can be surface or near-surface fishing under those feeding conditions.

Sizes in artificials in general should be pretty close to those of what they are supposed to imitate. These run between hook sizes 6 and 14, but a few tiny representations, such as midges, go as small as size 20. Don't be afraid of small sizes on fine leader tippets. It is amazing how clearly trout can see these tiny offerings and how quickly they take them!

DRY FLIES

When emerging nymphs shed their skins on the water's surface, thus transforming themselves into flying insects, they must float there momentarily while their wings expand and harden. Fish wait near the surface in feed

Shaking out line prevents drag in downstream drift. This angler is drifting a stonefly nymph on a western river. To prevent drag on the drift quartering downstream, he pulls back on the rod on completion of the forward cast so the line and leader drop in a series of S-curves. He can also extend the drift by shaking line out of the rod guides.

lanes and holding positions and avidly suck in the helpless insects. Hatches occur during clement months, but usually in afternoon or evening when the sun has warmed the water. Then, anglers try to imitate whatever is emerging with artificials of the same size and appearance and enjoy added thrills of seeing their floating representations taken on the surface.

While dry-fly fishing is best during hatches, it may be good when there aren't any. If insect representations don't do well then, try terrestrial ones like grasshoppers, ants and bees. We don't always need to be fussy about "matching the hatch" because a general representation often does as well as anything else if it is presented properly in suitable size. There are thousands of species and subspecies of flying insects which can be imitated, and hatches of several of them may occur at the same time. Thus a single general representation can take trout during any kind of hatch.

One such, which I have used successfully for years, is the Nearenuf, discussed in *The Sportsman's Notebook,* by my old friend, H. G. (Tap) Tapply. He and some of his fishing cronies decided to develop a dry fly which blended elements of several popular imitations such as the Quill Gordon, Red Quill and its female the Hendrickson, March Brown, Gray Fox and Light Cahill. While the composite wouldn't exactly imitate any of them, they thought it would be "near enough" to fool fish. It is, when used in proper size to match the hatching flies, which most often are 14s or 16s. Bordering sizes 12s and 18s also are useful. The dressing is:

> *Wings:* A strip of wood-duck side feather, split and upright
> *Hackle:* Mixed dark ginger and grizzly
> *Body:* A quill from a peacock's eye feather
> *Tail:* Two stripped grizzly hackle barbules, flared and tied extra long

While selections in dry flies can be oversimplified, the tendency of novice anglers is to trust the blandishments of merchants and to stock too many. Size is more important than pattern. If rising fish don't strike the pattern you are using, tie on a smaller one.

In dry-fly fishing the line and fly should float and the leader should sink. Modern lines offer no floating problem if they are kept clean. Flies can be dried in the air, but spraying them with a floatant coating helps. There are preparations which make leaders sink, but soap, fish slime or mud can do it. The important thing is to use a properly tapered leader, nine feet long, or more, with a tippet suitable in size to the fly. Coils can be removed by holding the leader taut and by rubbing it back and forth vigorously with a doubled piece of innertube rubber or a piece of soft leather to create frictional heat. Connect fly to leader with a Turle Knot.

Excellently matched tackle and the ideal choice of fly mean nothing if the cast is clumsy. Aim a few feet *above* the target so fly and leader will straighten and flutter down without splash. Also aim a few feet *upstream* of the target so the fly will drift into position. Also cast a few feet *beyond* the target so the rod can be pulled back a bit after the line has extended to make the line and leader drop in a series of S-curves to prevent drag during the drift. Drag can later be decreased by mending the line when necessary.

Upstream Casting

Upstream casting with the dry fly is the time-honored method, but you must cast a bit to the right or to the left so the leader won't pass over the fish. Since fish face upstream, your approach from behind is less obvious, particularly if you're wading with a low silhouette. The fly will drift toward you with minimum drag, and you must strip in line fast enough to be in control to strike a rising fish. The strip-in should never pull the fly. Since the strike is from downstream, with the fish facing upstream, the hook is pulled into the apex of the fish's jaws, where it should be. Another advantage of upstream fishing is that fish farther upstream are not disturbed.

The British usually wait for rising fish and cast to selected ones. Of course we do that, too, but we also fish blindly, aiming casts so the fly will pass over or into potential holding positions or down feed lanes. Upstream casting can be any combination of up and across. When it is more across than up, drag on the fly can be postponed not only by checking the cast but also by wiggling the rod from side to side to shoot out extra line into a more pronounced series of S-curves. The line of course is mended as often as necessary.

Other suggestions for making fish strike: Get into the stream whenever possible, to maintain a low silhouette. Try to keep in position relative to the sun so your shadow won't disturb the fish. Fish slowly to minimize shock waves. When trout are rising out of reach, the nearer ones have heard or seen the angler because he isn't fishing slowly enough. Most fish can be taken within thirty feet. Too long a line only increases drag. When a trout rises but rejects the fly, this may be because of drag rather than incorrect pattern or size. A smaller fly may be needed. The leader tippet should be adjusted to the size of the fly. Don't avoid tying on finer tippets. If the leader piles up it may need to be shortened.

In fast water my favorite dry flies include the Rat Faced MacDougal and the Irresistible, partly because of their superior floatability. Use the one you can see best. Wulff patterns also are excellent floaters. When fish are feeding in riffles, and when there is no reason for a different selection, try a Quill Gordon or a Light Cahill. In calm water my favorites include the Blue Dun Spider and the Cream Variant, which is a spider with wings. Sizes 14 or 16 should be about right. Spiders are tied on bare hooks with very wide spade hackles from a rooster's throat; two hackles with concave sides together. It is hard to land them poorly because they are air-resistant and flutter down. They skate enticingly in the slightest breeze.

This brings up the suggestion that strikes often can be coaxed by putting life into the fly in calm water. When a fly has hatched and its wings have hardened, it rarely rises into the air directly. It runs on the water for takeoff speed much like a duck does, leaving a tiny wake behind. This can be simulated, and trout seem to go for flies that are trying to escape. Some insects, such as stoneflies, are swimmers whose action can be duplicated to simulate the living insect. Terrestrials, including grasshoppers, ants and

Upstream casting with the dry fly. Angler notices a shady pocket
formed by two fallen trees and brush at A and another at B. To float
fly into position A, he would cast to the end of the log and allow the
fly to float into the pocket. The better position is the hiding place
under the log at B. Angler would cast well above the position to
drift the fly into the pocket (X).

bees, swim on the surface. An excellent way to trigger strikes is to cast a
Muddler dry so it floats, and to make it swim like a grasshopper with tiny
twitches of the rod tip. If a lunker lies below he should come for it.

Downstream Casting
While upstream dry-fly fishing is the traditional method, it is often more
convenient to fish downstream. Wind direction or the sun's position may
influence this. Wading downstream requires less exertion than trying to
wade up, and fast water may make it mandatory. Casts nearly downstream
present the fly without the fish seeing the leader. Many positions can be

fished downstream much better than up. We read the water and decide each situation on its merits.

Downstream casting of course requires more loose line to obtain a suitable float, and it may require mending the line frequently. Pulling back on the rod as the cast straightens out lands the line in S-curves which provide a short float without drag, and shaking out more line also may be necessary.

Downstream fishing is at its best in slow-flowing water. An ideal situation then may be a combination of both up and down, such as to cover a run along an undercut bank or the upstream side of a submerged rock and the edges below it. Aim the cast quartering upstream and mend while the fly works downstream, providing additional line as need be.

The Dry Fly on Fast Water
Many smaller streams run fast, but big trout, especially rainbows, can abound in them. Light tackle is preferable because thick lines offer greater water resistance and thus tend to drag. Since casts must be short because of the broken currents, a double-tapered line is preferable to a forward-tapered one. Light tackle with light lines permit using lighter leaders for freer fly movement and less drag. This light tackle, with short casts, still allows wading anglers to probe many holding positions; perhaps all of them on the smaller streams. When rivers are wider and also very fast, the dry fly may be unsuitable.

Casts in fast water must be short and frequent. Long leaders help to keep flies floating. The sneaky approach is less important because the disturbed surface obscures anglers from fish. The rough surface also decreases fly visibility, making pattern less important but increasing the necessity for color contrast. Rocky stretches offering promising edges and holding water can probably be fished most effectively by working upstream, but downstream fishing should usually be more practical.

Of course dry flies for fast water must have extreme buoyancy to float high. Wulff patterns and those with clipped deer-hair bodies are ideal. They will often be pulled under but the cast can then be completed wet.

BASS BUGS AND SIMILAR FLOATERS

In addition to flies, artificials for the fly rod include a vast and potent array of deer-hair, cork and plastic floaters excellent for all the basses and for surface-feeding panfish. Lunker trout (especially brown trout) shouldn't be excluded, particularly when we fish for them at night. These lures include lightweight poppers of many sorts and sizes as well as representations of mice, frogs, moths, bugs and anything else landing on the surface which fish consider suitable for dinner.

Depending on the size and air-resistance of the lure, rods can vary in size—from lightweight rods taking line size 6 to heavier ones taking size 10. Since all of these lures are air-resistant to some degree, a weight-forward floating line is needed to cast them properly. For the big lures, a bass-bug taper, made particularly for the purpose, should be chosen. We can be less particular about the leader for casting the bigger lures, but it should be about as long as the rod and should gradually taper from about 12 to 8

Dry-fly fishing on fast water. Rocky water like this looks too fast for good fishing, but it contains pockets above and behind boulders where flow is moderate. Such spots often harbor big fish. Since floats are short before drag sets in, casts must be frequent. Drop a good floater in the same spot many times, allowing it to drift only a foot or two, to simulate a hatch.

pounds. A strong tippet is needed to turn the bulky lures over, and is acceptable because the fish with which we are concerned are less fussy than trout. A strong leader is required because much of this fishing is amid pads, grasses, stumps, brush and other obstructions from which hooked fish must be pulled quickly. Weedless hooks are usually valuable.

Popping lures are fished by allowing them to lie quietly after the cast, then given noisy pops and gurgles by pulling the rod tip back sharply. This noise and surface commotion wakes up lethargic bass and usually elicits lusty strikes.

Except for poppers and bullet heads, nearly all of these lures imitate naturals. In addition to casting the lures to potential hot spots, you must work the lure exactly as its live counterpart swims; *don't hurry or overdo it.* Let's stress this with a few examples.

We'll use a little green deer-hair frog with splayed legs; an excellent lunker bass lure. Cast it onto or very close to a lily pad or stump or some such place from which a frog might jump, and *leave it alone* for at least half a minute. We can imagine a big bass lying below making up his mind whether or not to strike. Give the lure the slightest possible teasing twitch. Wait a few seconds. Give it a slightly stronger twitch. Wait again. If nothing happens, make the frog swim slowly in short jerks with alternating pauses until the cast is fished out. If a bass or pickerel sees the lure, he should take it. Watch small frogs to see how they act in the water, and fish their counterparts exactly the same way. Novice anglers usually discourage strikes by hurrying the action too much.

Big bass love mice. Big trout do, too. Little gray or black fly-rod mice with bodies only an inch or so long plus a rubberband tail are made of closely cropped deer body hair, and are therefore very buoyant. Mice often fall off logs, or try to swim from one place to another. Unlike frogs, they paddle steadily but very slowly on the surface, leaving small, enticing wakes. Fish the lure steadily and slowly, perhaps with a few pauses.

Due to insecticides moths are less prevalent than they used to be, but bass don't seem to realize that. A moth flutters steadily over the surface, like a float plane getting speed for takeoff. Fly-rod moths are made of cropped deer hair, with wide and long horizontal wings. Fish them with the mouse treatment, but perhaps a little faster.

These four fly-rod artificials are all that seem necessary for largemouth bass, and smallmouths may take the same lures in smaller sizes. If they don't, they may not be in the shallows, and we'll have to look for them in deeper structure. We know that bass habitually move into the shallows to feed between dusk and dawn when the water is in a temperature range comfortable for swimming. In some regions, particularly in the South, they may be in the shallows most of the time.

Smallmouth bass fishing is more akin to trouting than to largemouth fishing, partly because smallmouths shun weedy places for rocky or gravely ones. Their diet is insects and their nymphs, terrestrials such as moths, beetles and hoppers, crayfish, and small baitfish. Since insects which have fallen into the water are drifted by winds to the windward shore, the feeding pattern of smallmouths is more pronounced there.

Thus, smallmouths take fly-rod lures which have been mentioned for trout. I have two favorite floaters for them. One is the ever-popular Muddler Minnow fished dry, like a grasshopper, or a real grasshopper imitation. Another is a deer-hair bug, such as the Cooper Bug. It can be deadly for rising smallmouths when fished properly. This means to land it delicately and to let it sit without motion for nearly a minute. Then give it just the faintest twitch, followed by a few more. If there are no takers, pick it up and drop it in another place. Here again the imitation must be fished as the natural would act. Rubber bugs, caterpillars, grubs, ants, bees and tiny popping lures also are excellent floaters for smallmouths and for many other panfish. Good hook sizes are from 4 to 6.

Bluegills (bream) are favorites among the panfishes which feed on insects. Try them with light fly rods and fine leaders using any of the midget-sized lures just discussed for smallmouths. Best results come when the little lures are fished along shorelines with cover in early morning or during the evening when the sun is off the water. We may have to experiment to find out which type of lure takes best at any one time, but that is part of the fun. Whatever it is, the secret is to fish it as its living counterpart would act on the water.

In my last book, *Fishing* (Outdoor Life, E. P. Dutton), I covered the basic tackle and tactics for taking the most popular fresh- and saltwater gamefish in North America. "Make the new one a graduate course," my editor said. "Provide information that will help anglers determine where fish should be found, and how to make them strike." The assignment has been fun, and I hope it will be of service. To avoid repetition as much as possible, and to keep this book within reasonable length, I have assumed that readers understand the basics.

Needless to say, a complete graduate course in angling would include the many specialized books on the subject, some contemporary, others old and revered classics. Knowledgeable anglers increase their enjoyment of the sport by reading the lore of the past as well as by studying the facts and opinions of the present.

Specialized books, written by the world's greatest anglers, describe how to select and fish wet flies, dry flies, nymphs, streamers and other lures, each subject meriting perhaps several books of its own from which readers can accept or reject the authors' advice, as their judgment dictates. Other specialized books treat with fishing for trout, bass, steelhead or salmon. Still others deal with entomology, tackle making, stream improvement, fly dressing.

Certainly, one of the required subjects of any graduate course is contained in this book, for reading the water to understand the habits of fish, and why they strike or why they don't, is of primary importance to student anglers. We hope this information will be as valuable to them as it has been to me.

Index